SALUTING AMERICAN
VALOR

SALUTING AMERICAN VALOR

Selfless courage at the moment of truth

Stephens Press ✳ Las Vegas, Nevada

Editor: Stephan R. Tetreault
Designer: Sue Campbell
Publishing Coordinator: Stacey Fott

Cataloging in Publication
Saluting American valor: selfless courage at the moment of
truth / edited by Stephan R. Tetreault ; foreword by Warren
Stephens ; preface by Gen. Peter Pace, USMC (ret.).
220 p.: ill., photos ; 20 cm.

ISBN: 1-935043-17-X
ISBN-13: 978-1-935043-17-1

Compiles the fifty-four part newspaper series that tells the
stories of heroism and bravery by the men and women in the
United States Armed Forces serving in Iraq and Afghanistan
who have received medals of honor.

1. Military decorations—United States. 2. United States.
Armed Forces—Iraq. 3. United States. Armed Forces—
Afghanistan. I. Tetreault, Stephan R., ed. II. Stephens,
Warren. III. Pace, Peter.

355.134'092 dc22   2010   2009943284

STEPHENS PRESS, LLC
A Stephens Media Company

Post Office Box 1600
Las Vegas, NV 89125-1600
www.stephenspress.com

Printed in Hong Kong

"This is as true in everyday life as it is in battle: we are given one life and the decision is ours whether to wait for circumstances to make up our mind, or whether to act, and in acting, to live."

—General Omar Bradley

This book is dedicated to all men and women who have served in uniform to carry out Operation Enduring Freedom and Operation Iraqi Freedom.

CONTENTS

★★★
6
★★★

Contributors

FOREWORD

THE IDEA FOR THIS BOOK ORIGINATED ONE AFTERNOON when talking to one of my associates. His father had passed away recently and, being a World War II veteran, had been buried in Arlington National Cemetery.

It turns out he also had won Silver and Bronze stars during his service in Europe. I asked to read the commendation recounting the action that led to his Silver Star and was simply amazed at what this man had done.

It then hit me that these same types of situations were taking place in Iraq and Afghanistan and that we should tell those stories.

So we are privileged and humbled to offer this book that tells the stories of heroism and bravery by the men and women in the United States Armed Forces.

Their differences are striking by any measure — age, ethnicity, background and experience: the forklift driver from rural Arkansas who doubles as an Army National Guard captain after serving six years in the Air Force; the flight instructor and chief warrant officer from Reno, the Biggest Little City in the World; the Army Reserve private who normally is a salesman in a small town northwest of Houston.

Some are citizen soldiers, who helped change the misguided image of the Guard and Reserves from the oft-maligned

"Weekend Warrior" to a status that properly honors them as critical to our nation's fighting force. Others chose the military as a career.

Their dissimilarities, however, end here. All left the safety of home and family, often more than once, to serve their country with distinction: In the searing heat and blowing sands of Iraq, never knowing if a hidden explosive, suicide bomber or ambush awaits them just a few clicks down the road; in the mountains of Afghanistan, where hidden fortresses and tunnels existed for decades (if not centuries) in a land that never has been conquered by a foreign force.

Some saw the horrors in both countries. But all, in their moment of truth, displayed a selfless bravery in combat that most people simply cannot comprehend.

Since 2001, more than 1.9 million Americans have served at least one tour of duty in Iraq and/or Afghanistan. War is tragic and frightening. Some 4,500 Americans and thousands of civilians and enemy insurgents have died. And too many U.S. soldiers have come home with life-altering wounds, both physical and psychological.

But at key moments, when faced with life-or-death situations, many responded in extraordinary ways, saving not only their own lives but those of comrades and civilians.

Some of their stories have been told elsewhere. Others have not. We searched for soldiers, sailors, airmen and Marines whose stories of valor were representative of those who have served. Many of their stories are recounted in their own words.

Most heroes do not seek the spotlight, and in fact, many we contacted declined the attention, leaving their stories untold.

We tell these stories because we must. Sometimes lost in the political rhetoric — and in diminished interest that can come from prolonged military engagements — is the fact that fellow Americans put themselves on the line and perform stunning acts of courage.

We thank them for sharing their stories. Truly, they are the heroes among us. ★

– Warren Stephens
Chairman, President and
Chief Executive Officer, Stephens Inc.

★ ★ ★
9
★ ★ ★

★★★
10
★★★

PREFACE

What is a Hero? by General Peter Pace, USMC (Retired)

WHO'S YOUR HERO? We often respond to such a question with the name of a talented actor, gifted athlete, generous philanthropist, charismatic leader or perhaps a famous historical figure. Sometimes we use the word "hero" to describe our admiration and appreciation for those who have broken a world record, overcome personal obstacles to accomplish greatness or even enriched our lives with an act of kindness.

Heroism is more than talent, success, generosity, strength or determination. Heroes emerge when courage and selflessness combine, resulting in amazing acts that serve others.

Our nation's men and women in uniform demonstrate real heroism every day. Quite simply the finest armed forces in the world, these incredible warriors put their lives on the line to defend the freedoms we all hold dear.

With a full understanding of exactly what service to this nation means – often facing repeated deployments to Iraq and Afghanistan – these young men and women raise their right hands and continue to serve with exceptional courage and selflessness. They remain committed to making a difference, choosing to be part of something bigger than self.

This level of dedication cannot be ordered or demanded, it can only be given. Their gift will ensure that our children, and our children's children, enjoy the same freedoms that Americans have enjoyed since the birth of this nation.

That gift of service simply would not be possible without our military families, who offer quiet strength and untold support. Through long deployments, they sustain morale from afar while maintaining the family foundation at home, despite daily challenges and unspoken worries. Our military families serve this nation as well as anyone who has ever worn a uniform, and for that we are eternally grateful.

★ ★ ★

11

★ ★ ★

True heroes do not consider the title appropriate. They often describe their personal feats as "just doing my job" – a "job" that makes our other hero-worshipping possible.

This book offers a closer view of just a few of these heroes. By highlighting the courageous and selfless actions of our dedicated military personnel, we honor their service and demonstrate our gratitude.

To our heroes in uniform: Thank you. America values your courage, character and sense of duty.

ACKNOWLEDGMENTS

THIS BOOK WOULD NOT HAVE BEEN POSSIBLE BUT FOR the men and women who agreed to talk about some of the most intense experiences of their lives. Hopefully this book does them justice.

It also would not have been possible without the representatives of the armed forces who helped locate the soldiers, sailors, Marines and airmen who were sought for interviews. Thanks to First Lieutenant Joshua Diddams of the U.S. Marine Corps; Major Corey E. Schultz of the U.S. Army Reserve; Captain Paul L. Greenberg of the U.S. Marine Corps Reserve; Major Paul Villagran of the U.S. Air Force; and information officers at military installations around the country and in Europe.

Thanks also to Wayne V. Hall of the U.S. Army; Lieutenant Colonel Mike Moose and Master Sergeant Keith O'Donnell of the U.S. Army Human Resources Command; and Cherish T. Washington, Elizabeth Lacquement and Jenn Domashevich of U.S. Army Public Affairs.

Thanks to Warren Stephens for the idea of spotlighting modern day military heroes, and for urging the idea be brought to life.

Thanks to Sherman Frederick for granting editors and writers the time to do a thoughtful job.

Thanks to the writers, photographers and videographers who embraced this project with commitment and enthusiasm, and in particular to Andrew Lubin, who saw its potential from the start and who was generous in sharing his expertise.

Thanks to the skilled staffs of the *Las Vegas Review-Journal* and the Arkansas News Bureau who dedicated themselves to the project alongside their daily assignments. Thanks to in-house military expert Keith Rogers, to Tonya Carpenter for designing and maintaining the project website; and to audio/video producer Michael Quine.

Thanks to copy editor Steve Blust and a special thanks to Charlie Waters for his wise counsel. ★

— **Steve Tetreault**
Saluting American Valor, Editor
Bureau Chief, Stephens Washington News Bureau

★ ★ ★
13
★ ★ ★

Photo by Staff Sergeant Angelita Lawrence DOD

THE MEDALS

U.S. Military Decorations

Distinguished Service Cross

THE DISTINGUISHED SERVICE CROSS is the second-highest military decoration that can be given to a member of the U.S. Army, awarded for extreme gallantry and risk of life in combat with an armed enemy force. Actions that merit the Distinguished Service Cross must be of such a high degree to be above those required for all other U.S. combat decorations but not meeting the criteria for the Medal of Honor.

Air Force Cross

THE AIR FORCE CROSS IS THE SECOND-highest military decoration that can be awarded to a member of the U.S. Air Force. It is awarded for extraordinary heroism not justifying the award of the Medal of Honor. It may be awarded to any person who, while serving in any capacity with the Air Force, distinguishes himself or herself by extraordinary heroism in combat.

Navy Cross

THE NAVY CROSS IS THE SECOND-HIGHest award that can be given for valor to members of the U.S. Navy, Marine Corps and Coast Guard. The Navy Cross also could be awarded to all branches of U.S. military and members of foreign militaries.

Silver Star

THE SILVER STAR IS THE THIRD-highest military decoration that can be awarded to a member of any branch of the U.S. Armed Forces. It is also the third-highest award given for valor in the face of the enemy. The Silver Star is awarded for gallantry in action against an enemy of the United States not justifying a Service Cross.

Distinguished Flying Cross

THE DISTINGUISHED FLYING CROSS IS a medal awarded to any officer or enlisted member of the U.S. Armed Forces who distinguishes himself or herself in support of operations by heroism or extraordinary achievement while participating in an aerial flight.

Bronze Star with Valor

THE BRONZE STAR IS AWARDED FOR bravery, acts of merit or meritorious service. When awarded for bravery it is distinguished by the "V" attachment. It is the fourth-highest combat award of the U.S. Armed Forces and the ninth-highest military award (including both combat and non-combat awards) in the order of precedence of U.S. military decorations.

Purple Heart

THE PURPLE HEART IS AWARDED IN THE NAME OF THE President of the United States to any member of an Armed Force who has been wounded or killed or who has died or may die after being wounded:

(1) In any action against an enemy of the United States;

(2) In any action with an opposing armed force of a foreign country in which the U.S. Armed Forces are or have been engaged;

(3) While serving with friendly foreign forces engaged in an armed conflict against an opposing armed force in which the United States is not a belligerent party;

(4) As a result of an act of any such enemy of opposing armed forces; or

(5) As the result of an act of any hostile foreign force.

★★★

15

★★★

The Medal of Honor

Stories by Brian Mockenhaupt

THEY KNEW THEY WOULD PROBABLY DIE. HOW COULD they not? Still, they dived on grenades, darted into gunfire to save wounded comrades and beat back enemy attacks. And for those actions, on the sun-baked streets of Iraq and in the rugged mountains of Afghanistan, they received a Medal of Honor, the United States' highest award for bravery.

"They were willing to go to the extreme of putting themselves in jeopardy to save someone else," says Dan Murphy, father of Navy SEAL and medal recipient Michael Murphy. "I don't think it gets any more honorable than that."

Created by Congress in 1862 to recognize valorous conduct, the Medal of Honor has been awarded 3,468 times. Nineteen men received it twice. One woman, Dr. Mary Edwards Walker, received the medal, in 1865 for her services as a Civil War nurse at the first Battle of Bull Run.

Nearly half the medals were awarded during the Civil War, when it was one of the country's few military recognitions. Since then, as criteria became more stringent and lesser medals for valor were introduced, the Medal of Honor has grown in prominence and exclusivity.

Just six have been awarded for actions in Afghanistan and Iraq, all to men mortally wounded in battle.

According to legislation that created the medal, "The deed performed must have been one of personal bravery or self-sacrifice so conspicuous as to clearly distinguish the individual above his comrades and must have involved risk of life."

The award process, which requires statements by at least two eyewitnesses, can take two years.

There have been relatively few medals awarded in recent years — and all posthumously.

Part of the explanation for the relatively small number of Medals of Honor is the evolution of American warfare. New technologies such as aerial drones and precision-guided bombs allow commanders to engage enemy forces from a distance and keep more soldiers out of harm's way.

"Additionally, the war is against non-uniformed insurgents who inflict damage on U.S. personnel by using tactics and techniques that reduce their risk of being personally engaged," according to Lietenant Cololnel Les Melnyk, a Defense Department spokesman.

"The enemy minimizes their risk by using remotely detonated improvised explosive devices, suicide bombers, and rocket, mortar and sniper attacks."

The vast majority of U.S. deaths and injuries in Iraq and Afghanistan have been caused by IEDs, according to the Defense Manpower Data Center.

But while there may be less close-quarters combat than in past wars, there are still many moments on today's battlefields when service members weigh a deadly question: Will they sacrifice their own lives to save others?

The following six men received the Medal of Honor for their heroic actions in Afghanistan or Iraq. ★

VALOR

There are three present day variations of the Medal of Honor. The medal at the center is for the Air Force, while the medal on the left is for the Army, and the the one at right is for the Navy and Marine Corps.

Jason L. Dunham
U.S. Marine Corps

Died April 22, 2004

INSURGENTS HAD JUST AMBUSHED A MARINE CONVOY NEAR Karabilah, Iraq, on April 14, 2004, and Corporal Jason Dunham's squad was searching a line of vehicles fleeing the area.

As Dunham approached a white Toyota Land Cruiser, the driver leaped from the truck and wrestled with Dunham. A moment later, an explosion ripped through the air, wounding Dunham and two other Marines of 2nd squad, 4th Platoon, Kilo Company, 3rd Battalion, 7th Marines.

When Kilo's commander, Captain Trent Gibson, arrived at the scene a few minutes later, he found pieces of Dunham's helmet strewn across the street. But he didn't know the full story until the next day.

Lance Corporal Jason Sanders — the fourth Marine near the explosion — told Gibson about a conversation a couple of weeks earlier: Several Marines had been talking about what they would do if a grenade landed near them. Dunham figured he could cover the grenade with his helmet to absorb the blast.

No way, his platoon leader, Second Lieutenant Brian Robinson, said. It couldn't be done fast enough.

Time me, Dunham said. In about a second, he scooped the helmet from his head and slammed it onto the ground.

Gibson now understood why the explosion shredded the helmet: Dunham had smothered the blast.

"He always looked after others before he looked after himself," Gibson says. "So that was a very natural thing for him to do, to cover up that grenade in order to protect the Marines around him. He was the kind of guy you'd want to have in charge of your son. He was a man of character, and he led not by intimidation but by example."

Dunham died on April 22, 2004, at Bethesda Naval Medical Hospital in Maryland. He is credited with saving the lives of two Marines.

"One of those Marines is now the proud father of a three-year-old girl," Gibson says. "It's been a gift that keeps on giving, not only in creating more lives but in providing an example of selflessness for Marines now and God knows how many Marines in the future.

"Through his story, they can be inspired to be that kind of person."

★ ★ ★

Corporal Jason L. Dunham, twenty-two, was born in Scio, New York, on November 10, 1981 — also the Marine Corps' birthday. He joined the Marines in 2000 and deployed to Iraq in early 2004 as a squad leader with 4th Platoon, Kilo Company, 3rd Battalion, 7th Regiment, 1st Division, 1 Marine Expeditionary Force. He was wounded in Karabilah, Iraq, on April 14, 2004. ★

Deb Dunham, mother of Medal of Honor recipient Jason Dunham, holds a portrait of her Marine son in uniform. Below left: Sergeant Mark Dean — one of Medal of Honor recipient Corporal Jason Dunham's close friends — and Captain Trent Gibson, Dunham's former company commander, sort out the pieces of the Kevlar helmet Dunham used to help absorb the blast of a grenade in the streets of Iraq in 2004.

19

Ross A. McGinnis
U.S. Army

Died December 4, 2006

THE HUMVEE WOUND THROUGH THE WARREN OF STREETS in the Adhamiyah section of Baghdad, and Specialist Ross McGinnis scanned the rooftops and alleyways from the turret. The threats were many, and as the gunner, he was the eyes and ears for the four soldiers sitting below.

Adhamiyah, wracked by sectarian violence, had become a particularly deadly neighborhood for U.S. troops. Insurgents buried massive bombs in the roads, fired at patrols from windows and popped out of alleyways with rocket-propelled grenades.

"It was a nasty fight," says Sergeant First Class Cedric Thomas, First Platoon Sergeant of Charlie Company, First Battalion, 26th Infantry Regiment. The company already had lost two soldiers, two of 14 killed during the 15-month deployment. Dozens more were wounded.

On December 4, 2006, the six-truck patrol rolled through the neighborhood to deliver a generator to residents. McGinnis rode in the last Humvee. From a rooftop, an insurgent pitched a grenade toward the truck. McGinnis tried to bat it away, but it hit the roof, fell inside and landed with a clang against the radio mount between the driver, Sergeant Lyle Buehler, and Thomas, the passenger.

"Grenade!" McGinnis yelled

"Where?" Thomas asked.

"It's in the truck!"

Another grenade had been thrown into a Humvee several weeks earlier, but that one was a dud.

This one wasn't.

Before Thomas put his head between his legs and braced for the explosion, he saw McGinnis sit down, trapping the grenade between his body and the radio mount.

"He could have jumped out," Thomas says. "That's what he was trained to do. Alert the crew and jump out."

The doors blew open and the truck filled with black smoke. The grenade killed McGinnis instantly and wounded the four other soldiers.

"If Ross would have jumped out," Thomas says, "there would be four of us not here today."

When the platoon returned to the combat outpost that night, Thomas approached Captain Michael Baka, the company commander.

"Sir," he said, "McGinnis saved our lives today."

★ ★ ★

Specialist Ross A. McGinnis, nineteen, was born June 14, 1987, in Meadville, Pennsylvania, and grew up in Knox, Pennsylvania. He enlisted in the Army on his seventeeth birthday and deployed to Iraq in August 2006 with 1st Platoon, C Company, 1st Battalion, 26th Infantry Regiment, 2nd Brigade Combat Team, 1st Infantry Division. He was killed December 4, 2006.

★

★ ★ ★
20
★ ★ ★

Map of Iraq illustrates where Dunham, McGinnis, Monsoor, and Smith were killed.

Tal Afar · Mosul · Irbil · Kirkuk · Tikrit · Samarra · Karabilah Dunham · Balad · Baghdad Intl Airport Smith · Baghdad · Adhamiyah, Baghdad McGinnis · Hilt · Rutbah · Ramadi Monsoor · Fallujah · Karbala · Hillah · Kut · Kufah · Diwaniyah

Michael A. Monsoor
U.S. Navy

Died September 29, 2006

When Petty Officer Michael Monsoor arrived in Ramadi in April, 2006, the city was the most dangerous in Iraq for U.S. forces.

He and his teammates on SEAL Team 3 were attacked on 75 percent of their patrols through the city as they trained Iraqi soldiers. Monsoor, a machine gunner, had fired thousands of rounds during three dozen gun battles with insurgents.

On May 9, 2006, a SEAL near Monsoor was shot in the leg during a patrol and lay bleeding in the street. Monsoor ran to him as bullets kicked up dirt around him and dragged the wounded man to safety, an action for which he received the Silver Star. He also earned a Bronze Star with Valor for actions during eleven firefights with insurgents.

In e-mails home, he never told his family how much danger he faced each day.

On September 29, 2006, Monsoor, three other SEALs and eight Iraqi soldiers climbed onto a rooftop from which they could watch over soldiers pushing through a dangerous neighborhood. The SEAL snipers fired on several men with AK-47s, killing one and wounding another.

Over loudspeakers at a nearby mosque, insurgents were then called to attack. They fired at the rooftop with automatic weapons and rocket-propelled grenades.

A grenade tossed onto the rooftop smacked Monsoor in the chest and dropped him to the ground. Monsoor called out to the two SEALs nearby, but they had no time to move. Standing near the exit, Monsoor could have dived to safety.

Instead, he collapsed onto the grenade. The two teammates near him were injured, but he absorbed most of the blast.

"He never took his eye off the grenade. His only movement was down toward it," a SEAL who was on the roof that day said later in an interview with the Associated Press.

"He undoubtedly saved mine and the other SEALs' lives, and we owe him."

★ ★ ★

Petty Officer Second Class Michael Anthony Monsoor, twenty-four, was born April 5, 1981, in Long Beach, California, and grew up in Garden Grove, California. He enlisted in the U.S. Navy on March 21, 2001. He deployed to Iraq in April 2006 with Delta Platoon, SEAL Team 3, and was killed September 29, 2006.

23

Paul R. Smith
U.S. Army

Died April 4, 2003

Before leaving for the Middle East in early 2003, Sergeant First Class Paul Ray Smith penned a letter to his family.

"There are two ways to come home: stepping off the plane, and being carried off the plane," he wrote. "It doesn't matter how I come home, because I am prepared to give all that I am, to insure that all my boys make it home."

Three months later, just after dawn on April 4, 2003, Smith and the men of 2nd Platoon, Bravo Company, 11th Engineer Battalion, were guarding the main road into Baghdad International Airport. Iraqi soldiers, who had awakened to find U.S. forces in their midst, fired at them sporadically and soon organized a large assault.

The engineers had been constructing a holding area for several prisoners captured in an earlier firefight when they saw dozens more Iraqi soldiers maneuvering toward their position. When they attacked, Smith lobbed hand grenades and launched a shoulder-fired rocket at the advancing soldiers.

A mortar round and rocket-propelled grenade slammed into an armored personnel carrier, wounding three American soldiers. Smith helped pull out the three casualties, who were taken to a nearby aid station, already crowded with battle injuries.

He then climbed atop the damaged vehicle and raked the Iraqi soldiers with fire from the .50-caliber machine gun, the top half of his body exposed in the turret.

"If he hadn't pushed the fight right then, that aid station would have taken a walloping," says Captain Brian Borkowski, Smith's platoon leader at the time. "It would have been ugly."

Smith told Private Michael Seaman to feed him ammunition from the shelter of the personnel carrier, firing 400 rounds and beating back the attack before he was killed by a shot to the head.

"He didn't send other people to do it. He took it upon himself," Borkowski says. "That's the valorous part."

He had seen such action before from Smith.

A few days earlier, one of the platoon's personnel carriers drove into a minefield. Smith, on hands and knees in the sand, cleared the mines, then guided the vehicle to safety.

"He was always leading from the front," Borkowski says. "He wasn't pushing anybody else out into the danger. And if they were there, he was willing to go out and get them back."

★ ★ ★

Sergeant First Class Paul Ray Smith, thirty-three, was born September 24, 1969, in El Paso Texas. He grew up in Tampa, Florida, and enlisted in the Army in October 1989. He deployed to Kuwait in early 2003 and entered Iraq in March 2003, with 2nd Platoon, B Company, 11th Engineer Battalion, 3rd Infantry Division. Married with two children, he was killed April 4, 2003. He previously had deployed to the first Persian Gulf War, to Bosnia-Herzegovina and Kosovo. ★

Right, inset: David Smith cradles the Medal of Honor presented to him by President George W. Bush on behalf of his father, Sergeant First Class Paul Smith, on April 4, 2005, at the White House.

★ ★ ★
24
★ ★ ★

Jared C. Monti

U.S. Army

Died June 21, 2006

As machine-gun rounds crashed into rocks all around him, Sergeant First Class Jared Monti saw one of his men lying wounded and exposed in the middle of a fearsome insurgent ambush, deep in the mountains of Afghanistan.

Monti ran toward Private First Class Brian Bradbury to pull him to safety but was turned back by bursts of gunfire. He tried again, and again was turned back. Monti rose and ran a third time toward Bradbury.

"Would every man have the ability to muster the courage to do that? No. I don't believe they would," says Command Sergeant Major James Redmore, who first met Monti in 1998 when they served together in the 82nd Airborne.

On June 21, 2006, Monti was the assistant leader of a sixteen-man reconnaissance patrol from 3rd Squadron, 71st Cavalry, 3rd Brigade, 10th Mountain Division, moving through the rugged mountains of Nurestan province in northeastern Afghanistan.

Insurgents, who may have been alerted to the patrol's position by a re-supply helicopter, attacked just before nightfall. As many as fifty fighters fired down on the patrol from a wooded ridgeline with machine guns and rocket-propelled grenades.

After organizing a quick defense, Monti called in air support and artillery fire from nearby bases. Redmore, the 3rd Brigade sergeant major who listened to the fight unfold over the radio, says Monti's actions stalled the attack and prevented the small patrol from being overrun.

"I don't think anybody ever expects to do anything extraordinary," Redmore says. "They try to do their job every day the best they can. . . . They're being overwhelmed by an enemy force. He's calmly calling in fire, which breaks up the enemy force, and he's going out to try to retrieve one of his fallen comrades. He does it once, twice, a third time. Is it extraordinary? Absolutely."

On Monti's last attempt to reach Bradbury, an RPG exploded nearby, mortally wounding him. Another American, Staff Sergeant Patrick Lybert, died during the attack, and several more were wounded.

Bradbury, the soldier Monti was trying to save, died later, along with flight medic Staff Sergeant Heath Craig, who had been lowered by winch cable from a Medevac helicopter.

As Craig and Bradbury were being pulled up, the cable broke, and the two men fell to their deaths.

★ ★ ★

Sergeant First Class Jared Christopher Monti, thirty, was born September 20, 1975, in Abington, Massachusetts, and grew up in Raynham, Massachusetts. He enlisted in the Army in March 1993 and deployed to Afghanistan in February 2006 as a forward observer with Headquarters and Headquarters Troop, 3rd Squadron, 71st Cavalry Regiment, 3rd Brigade Combat Team, 10th Mountain Division. He was killed June 21, 2006. ★

Map of Afghanistan illustrates where
Monti and Murphy were killed.

★★★
28
★★★

With the exception of Hospital Corpsman Second Class Marcus Luttrell, third from right, all the Navy SEALs pictured here were killed on June 28, 2005, in Afghanistan. Pictured are, from left, Sonar Technician (Surface) Second Class Matthew Axelson, Senior Chief Information Systems Technician Daniel Healy, Quartermaster Second Class James Suh, Machinist's Mate Second Class Eric Patton and Medal of Honor awardee Lieutenant Michael Murphy.

Michael Murphy
U.S. Navy

Died June 28, 2005

SURROUNDED AND OUTNUMBERED, LIEUTENANT MICHAEL Murphy and his men were pinned down on an Afghan mountainside and running out of ammunition.

Petty Officer Danny Dietz was dead. Murphy and Petty Officer Matthew Axelson were wounded. They needed help, but Murphy couldn't get a signal on the satellite phone. He'd have to move farther up the mountain, away from the cover of rocks and trees and into the open. He started climbing into a savage storm of bullets.

At Murphy's funeral two weeks later, Vice Adm. Joseph Maguire approached Murphy's father, Dan. "My men did not go down easy," Maguire told him. "There were Taliban bodies and blood trails strewn all over the place."

Murphy's four-man SEAL reconnaissance team had been hunting a Taliban leader near the Pakistan border on June 28, 2005, when three goat herders discovered the team's hiding position. Murphy had let the men go, and within an hour the SEALs were attacked by dozens of Taliban fighters. If help didn't come soon, they would be overrun.

Murphy climbed atop a boulder, phone in hand. Bullets slammed into his back, and he tumbled off the rock. He picked up the phone and again moved to high ground. The call went through, and he relayed his team's position. He traded fire with Taliban fighters until he was shot again and killed.

Responding to the call for help, an MH-47 Chinook helicopter loaded with more SEALs roared over the mountains to rescue the men, but Taliban fighters shot it down with a rocket-propelled grenade, killing all sixteen men on board.

Axelson died on the mountainside. Marcus Luttrell, the only survivor from Murphy's team, was blown down the rock face by an RPG blast and badly wounded. He was found the next day by villagers, given shelter and rescued by U.S. forces six days later.

Luttrell, Axelson and Dietz received the Navy Cross.

"These were his brothers, and he would sacrifice his life for his brothers," Dan Murphy says. "Michael's philosophy was always that the only life worth living was one in service to others."

Lieutenant Michael Murphy, twenty-nine, was born May 7, 1976, in Smithtown, New York. He grew up in Patchogue, New York, and joined the Navy in September 2000, eventually serving with SEAL Delivery Vehicle Team One, based in Pearl Harbor, Hawaii. He deployed to Jordan, Qatar and Djibouti, then to Afghanistan in early 2005. He was killed in June 2005.

29

AFGHANISTAN WAR OVERVIEW

U.S. and coalition forces took the fight to Taliban and al-Qaida elements — to varying degrees — for most of a decade.

By Andrew Lubin

THE WAR BEGAN ON SEPTEMBER 11, 2001, IN NEW YORK City, at the Pentagon, and in a field in western Pennsylvania. On October 7, it moved to Afghanistan.

The United States and Great Britain launched a withering bombing campaign on military sites in Kabul, Jalalabad and Kandahar, strongholds of the Taliban movement that had given safe harbor to Osama bin Laden and his al-Qaida terrorist organization.

Within days, most Taliban training sites were severely damaged. In an omen of the years of fighting to come, however, thousands of fighters from the Pashtun ethnic group poured into the country from neighboring Pakistan, reinforcing the Taliban against the U.S.-led forces.

President George W. Bush and Secretary of Defense Donald Rumsfeld had decided to minimize the use of conventional Army forces. Therefore, the first American forces in Afghanistan came from the CIA's Special Activities Branch, with Army Special Forces joining them soon thereafter.

The plan was for the CIA and Special Forces to direct the anti-Taliban Northern Alliance in overthrowing the Taliban and al-Qaida. The goal was to capture bin Laden and other high-ranking al-Qaida members, destroy al-Qaida, and then remove and replace the Taliban with a friendly government.

Taking the fight to the Taliban

The ground fighting began on November 9 in the city of Mazar-i-Sharif. Bearded U.S. Special Forces soldiers on horseback, assisted by close-air support, directed the Northern Alliance into the city, where the Taliban fled after a bloody ninety-minute fight. Moving south, the Americans and their Northern Alliance troops reached Kabul on November 13, only to find that the Taliban had fled the city the previous night.

The fall of Kabul signaled the collapse of the Taliban. Within 24 hours, all of the Afghan provinces along the Iranian border had fallen. Local Pashtun commanders and warlords had taken over throughout northeastern Afghanistan, including the key city of Jalalabad.

Taliban holdouts in the north fell back to the northern city of Kondoz to make a stand. By November 16, Kondoz, the Taliban's last stronghold in northern Afghanistan, was besieged by the Northern Alliance.

Taliban forces had been split into three groups; the one in Kondoz; another in their heartland around Kandahar; and the third, including Osama bin Laden, which was believed to be holed up in a cave complex in the Tora Bora Mountains, 18 miles southwest of Jalalabad.

Then the fighting intensified. American and British bombers pounded Kondoz for nine days.

The bombing also continued in the Tora Bora Mountains. CIA and Special Forces operatives were already at work, enlisting and paying local warlords to join the fight and planning an attack on the two thousand al-Qaida and Taliban troops defending the Tora Bora complex.

At the same time, American conventional troops finally had landed. A Marine Expeditionary Unit under the command of Lieutenant General James Mattis was airlifted from the Gulf of Oman and established Camp Rhino in the desert south of Kandahar on November 25. This was the first strategic American foothold in Afghanistan. The first significant combat involving American forces occurred the next day when fifteen armored Taliban vehicles approached Camp Rhino; Marine helicopter gunships destroyed most of them.

Meanwhile, air strikes continued to pound Taliban positions inside Kandahar, where Mullah Omar, the Taliban leader, was holed up. He remained defiant; despite controlling only four of the thirty Afghan provinces, he called on his forces to fight to the death.

Capturing Kandahar

Kandahar was the last remaining Taliban stronghold, but it was besieged; nearly three thousand tribal fighters led by Hamid Karzai blockaded the east while cutting off Kandahar's supply routes from the north as the Marines took positions to the south and west.

By December 6, Omar signaled that he was ready to surrender Kandahar to tribal forces, but President Bush rejected his offer, so on December 7, Omar slipped out of Kandahar. Karzai's forces seized the city while the Marines took control of Kandahar Airport and patrolled the region from Camp Rhino.

Battle of Tora Bora

Finally the U.S. focus shifted to Tora Bora. Local tribal militias, paid and organized by Special Forces and CIA, began to mass for an attack as heavy bombing continued of suspected al-Qaida positions.

On December 2, a group of twenty Special Forces members was inserted by helicopter to support the operation, while al-Qaida fighters moved to higher fortified positions and dug in for the battle. Subjected to round-the-clock air strikes by the U.S., the al-Qaida forces agreed to a truce, but they then outbid the local forces the U.S. already had paid and slipped, bin Laden included, into Pakistan.

Operation Anaconda: 2002

Following a "loya jirga," or grand council, an interim Afghan government was established in Kabul under Karzai. But the Taliban and al-Qaida had not given up. Al-Qaida forces began regrouping in the Shahi-Kot Mountains of Paktia province throughout January and February 2002.

U.S. intelligence sources picked up this buildup and prepared a massive push to counter it. On March 2, 2002, U.S. and Afghan forces launched an offensive, despite the Taliban being entrenched at altitudes of more than ten thousand feet.

Using guerilla tactics, the Taliban opened fire on the U.S. and Afghan forces, then retreated back into their caves, By March 6, eight Americans and seven Afghan soldiers were killed, and reportedly four hundred opposing forces had been killed in the fighting. However, several hundred guerrillas escaped to the Waziristan tribal areas across the border in Pakistan.

During Operation Anaconda and other missions in 2002 and 2003, special forces from several western nations also were involved in operations. These included the Australian Special Air Service Regiment, the Canadian Joint Task Force 2, the German KSK, the New Zealand Special Air Service and the Norwegian Marinejegerkommandoen.

Renewed Taliban insurgency: 2003–2007

With President Bush withdrawing American forces in order to attack Iraq, the remnants of the Taliban regained their confidence and started to launch the insurgency that Mullah Omar had promised during his last days in power. As months passed, the attacks increased in frequency south of Kandahar. Dozens

U.S. Army Soldiers with the 1st Battalion, 187th Infantry Regiment, 101st Airborne Division (Air Assault), scan the nearby ridgeline for enemy movement during Operation Anaconda on March 4, 2002. (Photo by Specialist David Marck Jr.)

of Afghan government soldiers, non-governmental organization and humanitarian workers and several U.S. soldiers died in the raids, ambushes and rocket attacks.

More European and Canadian troops were sent south to replace the Americans. The British manned southern Afghanistan, with troops and helicopters from Australia, Canada and the Netherlands.

Southern Afghanistan faced the deadliest spate of violence in the country since 2001 as NATO troops battled resurgent militants. NATO forces fought intensely throughout the second half of 2006, achieving tactical victories over the Taliban, but did not have the troop strength to occupy the areas they had just liberated.

Renewed commitment: 2008–2009

In the first months of 2008, the number of American troops increased by more than 80 percent to 48,250 in June. Yet on June 13, Taliban fighters demonstrated their strength by attacking the Kandahar jail. The well-planned operation freed twelve hundred prisoners, four hundred of whom were Taliban. On July 13, a coordinated Taliban attack was launched on a base in Wanat, almost wiping out an Army unit. On August 19, French troops suffered their worst losses when a patrol was ambushed in Kapisa province.

In March 2009, President Barack Obama announced the deployment of almost twenty-one thousand more troops, including ten thousand Marines who deployed virtually immediately. In June, under Brigadier General Lawrence Nicholson, they launched Operation Khanjar, the biggest American operation since 2001. The previous American commander, General David McKiernan, was relieved and replaced by General Stanley

U.S. and Afghan forces fight the Taliban side by side in Barge Matal, Afghanistan, during Operation Mountain Fire, July 13, 2009. (Photo by Staff Sergeant Christopher Allison)

McChrystal, whose new strategy involved protecting the population. Nicholson agreed with that strategy. "We're going to be with the people," he said. "We're not going to drive to work, we're going to walk to work."

Complicating the situation was the August national election in which President Karzai was accused of stealing enough votes to avoid a run-off election, as well as McChrystal's August report that "the Taliban had gained the upper hand and NATO is not winning." He said he needed forty thousand more troops to avoid defeat.

In September, the International Council on Security and Development released a map showing that the Taliban had a "permanent presence" in 80 percent of the country. In December, President Obama announced a new strategy to counter the Taliban and strengthen the Afghanistan military. He would send in 30,000 troops, bringing the U.S. presence in Afghanistan to close to 100,000 forces. But the president said he would set a goal to bring them home beginning in July 2011. ★

34

Heroes in Afghanistan

Gregory Ambrosia

U.S. Army, Silver Star

By Brian Mockenhaupt

FIRST LIEUTENANT GREGORY AMBROSIA KNEW THE RISK. But despite his platoon's hand grenades and machine-gun fire, the Afghan insurgents continued to move closer. If the enemy gained the high ground, they would pick off his men.

So Ambrosia ordered American gun trucks down in the valley to unleash their heavy machine guns and automatic grenade launchers toward the mountainside — at his platoon's position.

Bullets snapped overhead and skipped off stones as he and his men tucked in tight behind the rocks. Grenades exploded a few feet away.

And their day was just beginning.

The platoon had flown into the Watapor Valley in eastern Afghanistan the night before and established observation posts halfway up the mountain on both sides of the valley. From there they could protect an American convoy arriving to meet with village elders the next morning.

By dawn on September 25, 2007, the soldiers of Able Company, 2-503rd, 173rd Airborne Brigade, were intercepting enemy radio traffic: Fighters were gathering weapons and massing for an attack.

Afghan insurgents often exaggerate over the radio, knowing U.S. soldiers are listening. A broadcast of a well-planned, complex attack by a force of one hundred might actually be a couple of fighters taking potshots.

But Ambrosia and his men knew not to underestimate the fighters in this valley. The platoon had come here once before, about three months earlier on the Fourth of July. When that firefight ended the next day, two Able company soldiers were dead and five had been wounded.

Now they heard more radio chatter. "They were talking about overrunning our position and trying to take us captive," said Ambrosia, then age twenty-five and Able Company's executive officer. "That was their goal."

Just after eight a.m., the insurgents attacked the trucks in the valley and Ambrosia's position. The key, he knew, was to keep them from flanking his position and gaining the high ground. The enemy moved closer. Ambrosia heard the firing positions change, creeping farther up the mountain. As usual, he couldn't see the enemy, but he estimated the force at thirty.

"I was over there for sixteen months, and there were some times that our company was in contact three times a day," Ambrosia says. "And there was (only) one time that I saw a person shooting at me. The rest of the time it was tracer fire coming from shadows."

After the firepower from the American Humvees stalled the attack, the insurgent machine-gun fire tapered, and the trucks left to evacuate two soldiers with gunshot wounds.

By that point, however, Ambrosia could call on all the firepower in that corner of Afghanistan — mortars, artillery, bombers, jet fighters and helicopter gun ships. The mountainside fell silent three hours later, after Ambrosia had raked the area around his position with thirteen bombs, eighty-two artillery rounds, one hundred fifty mortar rounds, a dozen Hellfire missiles and thousands of machine-gun and rifle rounds.

Navy Admiral Mike Mullen, chairman of the Joint Chiefs of Staff, awards the Silver Star to Army Captain Gregory Ambrosia at Korengal Outpost, Afghanistan, on July 11, 2008. (Photo by Chad J. McNeeley)

Over the radio, Ambrosia heard an insurgent tell others to go home and pray for those who had been killed.

A helicopter delivered the soldiers from the second observation post to Ambrosia's position, and the reunited platoon hiked five hours back to base camp. As they walked, they listened to radio chatter about insurgents planning to attack the patrol. Ambrosia ordered more artillery and mortar to hammer likely ambush spots.

Throughout the hillside fight and the long walk home, none of Ambrosia's soldiers were hurt. He knows it could have been far worse.

On July 11, 2008, Adm. Mike Mullen, chairman of the Joint Chiefs of Staff, awarded Ambrosia a Silver Star during a visit to the Korengal Outpost.

Two days later and a few miles away, two hundred insurgents attacked a platoon from the battalion's Chosen Company, killing nine U.S. soldiers and wounding twenty-seven.

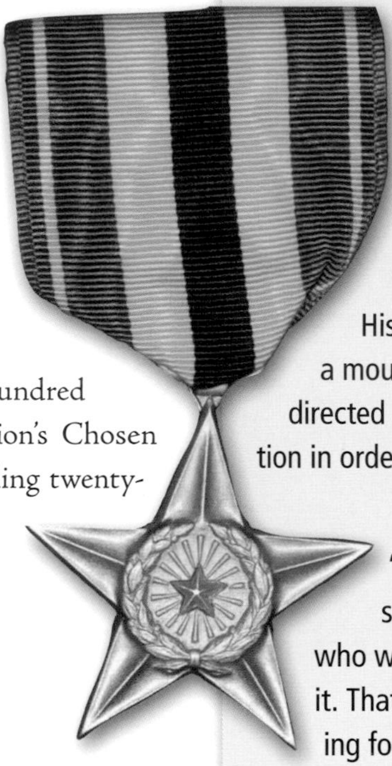

★★★
38
★★★

★

FIRST LIEUTENANT
Gregory Ambrosia
U.S. Army

- Born May 27, 1982, in Indianapolis. Moved at age five to Knoxville, Tennessee, where his family still lives.

- Entered West Point in June 2001, graduated May 28, 2005.

- Has served one fifteen-month tour in Afghanistan.

What he did

His platoon outnumbered and surrounded on a mountainside and with the enemy closing in, he directed American gunners below to fire on his position in order to buy time for help to arrive.

Why he joined the Army

"I had taken an American history class in high school where I learned about West Point, and who went there, and I was just really impressed with it. That was the gateway. It sounded really interesting for a young guy to be able to go out and do everything the Army lets you do. It seemed like an adventure."

Jason Amerine

U.S. Army, Bronze Star with Valor

By David Briscoe

THE TALIBAN ASSAULT FORCE ROLLED OUT OF A MOUNtain pass on November 16, 2001, about one thousand fighters headed toward a strategic town in south-central Afghanistan that had booted out local Taliban leaders.

From a ridge outside Tarin Kowt, capital of Oruzgan province, a ten-man U.S. Special Forces team, accompanied by a few dozen guerrillas and commanded by Captain Jason Amerine,

directed Navy F-18 air strikes against the approaching enemy convoy.

The day would be a roller coaster ride, one that would test Amerine's skills and emotions.

Suddenly, with American bombs blasting the enemy as it advanced, the guerrillas decided they'd had enough. They packed into their pickup trucks, threatening to leave the Americans stranded atop the ridge.

"All of us were yelling, trying to get them to stop, but we couldn't," Amerine recalled. With no choice but to jump aboard

Below: Captain Jason Amerine, second from right in the top row, worked closely with Pashtun tribal leader Hamid Karzai (third from right in the top row), who later ascended to the presidency in Afghanistan.

★★★
39
★★★

the pickups, "It was just an awful ride for thirty-five minutes as we retreated all the way back into town."

Two months after 9/11, in the early days of the war on terror, Amerine's tiny band of Green Berets had been dropped into Afghanistan to organize and train friendly locals. A resistance leader, Hamid Karzai, was trying to mobilize local fighters to oust Taliban radicals from the entire region around Tarin Kowt.

When they got back to town, Amerine told Karzai that the Americans needed to get back to the battle or the town would fall.

"So, we basically forced all the drivers out of their trucks, took the trucks, and we drove back out of town," Amerine said.

The Special Forces team returned to the ridge and called in more air strikes, confident they could still stop the Taliban advance.

But when the F-18s had to go back to reload, it was just Amerine and his nine men in pickup trucks against hundreds of Taliban, who couldn't be stopped.

"At one point, some of the lead elements of the enemy convoy got to the edge of town, and we heard small-arms fire," Amerine said. "That to me was it. The enemy made it to town. . . . We're going to have to start thinking about going and getting Karzai and getting out of there."

Then they realized the arms fire was coming not from the Taliban but from the Tarin Kowt residents.

"The people were engaging the (Taliban) convoy," Amerine said. "We still had hundreds of enemy coming for us, but the town was there fighting with us."

The day ended with an early victory in the war in Afghanistan. For Amerine, the battle led to a Bronze Star with Valor, making him one of the first decorated heroes of the war.

President Bush congratulates Jason Amerine.

For Karzai, it led to the Afghan presidency. The battle at Tarin Kowt established his credibility at home and abroad and turned the tide against the Taliban across the Pashtun tribal belt where the movement was born.

Just six weeks after Tarin Kowt, the Taliban surrendered Kandahar, Afghanistan's second-largest city. But Amerine and his team, with two men added, missed the surrender, falling victim just hours before to the deadliest friendly fire incident of the war.

Two men from Amerine's A-team, one other American and more than thirty Afghan guerrillas died when a soldier who had joined the operation with a headquarters group mistakenly called down a two thousand-pound bomb onto his own coordinates.

41

(Photo by Lucy Pemoni)

Amerine views the incident just north of Kandahar as part of the danger of war and calls the men killed in his unit — Master Sergeant Jefferson Davis of Clarksville, Tennessee, and Sergeant First Class Daniel Petithory of Cheshire, Massachusetts — the real heroes of the campaign.

In all, Amerine's unit received eleven Purple Hearts, eight Bronze Stars and two posthumous Silver Stars.

Amerine is the very image of a decorated soldier. If there's any doubt, his crouching, gun-wielding, square-jawed likeness has been molded in plastic as an Army action figure, and his electronic image is part of the Army's realistic military action game, America's Army.

Amerine is a consultant for the multiplayer computer game, which is a free download at www.americasarmy.com. ★

Captain
Jason Amerine
U.S. Army

- Born May 6, 1971, in San Gabriel, California. Family moved to Honolulu when he was three.

- Enrolled at the U.S. Military Academy at West Point in 1989, graduated in 1993 with a Bachelor of Science degree in Arabic, and was commissioned as a Second Lieutenant. Later, he earned a master's degree from Texas A&M University and taught international relations at West Point. Returned to Hawaii as a military strategist at U.S. Army Pacific Command.

- In Afghanistan, he was deployed with Operational Detachment Alpha-Team 574 within the 5th Special Forces Group (Airborne) from October to December 2001. A captain while serving in Afghanistan, he subsequently was promoted to major.

What he did
The Green Beret led a team of ten that coordinated air strikes to help defend a strategic town against a one thousand-strong convoy of Taliban fighters in the earliest days of the war in Afghanistan.

Why he joined the Army
"Growing up I was always interested in military service, so I don't really remember a time when I wasn't interested in joining the military."

A screen shot from the "America's Army" computer game featuring Amerine, and the Amerine action figure.

Stephen J. Boada
U.S. Marine Corps, Silver Star

By Dale Eisman

TWO OF HIS MARINES WERE DYING JUST A FEW FEET away, and gunfire all but pinned him to the ground. As he crouched behind a rock near the mouth of a cave, First Lieutenant Stephen James Boada could just about reach out and touch Lance Corporal Nicholas C. Kirven, felled by gunfire coming from inside.

Kirven was unresponsive, but Corporal Richard P. Schoener, wounded and bleeding nearby, was talking. Boada and Corporal Troy Arndt, crouched behind another rock, told Schoener to hold on.

It was May 8, 2005, Mother's Day. In Afghanistan's Alishang Valley, Boada and two squads of Marines dug into a hillside.

With bullets ripping into the ground and rock around him, Arndt managed to get a hand on Schoener and tried to pull him to cover, to no avail. Boada crawled over to help, but Schoener's flak vest ripped as the two Marines tugged at it.

The enemy gunmen, well sheltered in the cave, seemed to have plenty of ammunition. Boada tried tossing a smoke grenade into the entryway, hoping it would provide enough cover for a quick rescue. No good.

Boada had one fragmentation grenade. As Arndt and other Marines provided covering fire, Boada popped up above the rocks — fully visible to the enemy — and hurled the grenade into the cave. The fire kept coming. Arndt pulled another grenade off Schoener, and Boada popped up again to throw it.

Marines farther down the hill prepped other grenades and passed them forward. After the fourth blast, the cave went silent. Medics rushed forward to tend to Schoener and Kirven.

"No one's moving. No one's breathing," Boada recalled. "They just lost too much blood."

The Marines had hiked up and down a ridge more than six miles from an Afghan village in pursuit of the fighters in the cave. They were farther up the rugged and remote valley than coalition forces had previously penetrated. Now they had two fallen comrades to carry out. Bad weather made a helicopter pickup impossible.

And other enemy fighters were all over the area, tracking the Marines from a ridgeline and looking down on the platoon to plan and launch attacks.

An Afghan interpreter with the Marines overheard their chatter on the radio: The Americans would not get out alive, they said.

★★★
45
★★★

"It was ugly," recalled Boada, twenty-six at the time. "We tried just about every recovery technique the Marine Corps teaches you."

The Marines took turns carrying the bodies, fireman-style, over their shoulders. They fashioned litters from their ponchos, but none lasted long.

They commandeered two donkeys in one village. The terrain was so rugged, Boada said, "Even the donkeys, after about twenty minutes, they quit."

Several Marines, including Boada, were wounded. A citation accompanying the Silver Star he received months later describes how he "continued to fearlessly lead his Marines as they fought off a tenacious enemy while other members of the unit extracted their fallen comrades."

Boada shrugs off the award: "You get rewarded for doing your job."

As darkness arrived, the Marines overheard more enemy radio traffic: Ambushes were being set ahead. Boada twice called in AC-130 Spectre gunships, which were able to spot and shoot fighters who were preparing traps. His "tactical acumen in directing these aircraft saved many lives in the platoon," his award citation reads.

"We would have been in a tough spot, a much tougher spot if not for those guys," Boada said. "They did some phenomenal things for us." ★

★★★
46
★★★

First Lieutenant,
Stephen J. Boada
U.S. Marines

* Born December 19, 1978, in Bristol, Connecticut.

* Wife, Jennifer.

* An eleven-year Marine veteran, he served one tour in Iraq and one with the 1st Battalion, 12th Marines, in Afghanistan.

What he did
Fought off enemy gunmen in rugged terrain, allowing his squad to remove two Marines who had been killed in battle.

Why he joined the Marines
"I can't put my finger on it, but it was just something I always wanted to do."

James Brasher

U.S. Army, Silver Star

By Kevin Maurer

Standing atop a hill, he couldn't see the Taliban snipers shooting at him in the first light of day. Even after dropping several mortar rounds on their suspected locations, Sergeant First Class James Brasher knew his unit had to go into the village.

"It became clear we weren't going to get anything done unless we went down there," he said of the December 8, 2007, incident.

Brasher's unit had spent months clearing out the Helmand River Valley in Afghanistan. And U.S. coalition and Afghan forces had launched a final attack to clear Musa Qala, a village controlled by the Taliban for nine months.

The paratroopers had air-assaulted near the town and spent most of the night hiking to a large hill with a cell phone tower. They expected an attack that night, but the Taliban waited. Then, using a series of thick, mud-walled compounds and lush green fields as cover, the enemy opened fire at daybreak.

Brasher, a platoon sergeant from the 1st Battalion, 508th Parachute Infantry Regiment, and First Lieutenant Joseph McGovern led their platoon through the maze of compounds and irrigation ditches at the base of the hill. Taliban fighters waited, seemingly behind every corner, armed with machine guns and rocket-propelled grenades.

Rushing through a web of alleys, Brasher and his squad ran straight into a Taliban gunman, whom Brasher killed. Each time the paratroopers moved, they ran into more fire. Several times, Brasher hurled grenades so his men could find cover.

When McGovern's unit was attacked with machine-gun fire and RPGs, Brasher joined the other paratroopers. Taking his platoon to flank the gun site, Brasher's arm was shattered by a machine-gun burst.

"It was like I got whacked with something and it pushed me back and to the right," Brasher said. "I hit the ground and was screaming."

He continued barking orders, and medics had to force him to submit to care. He desperately wanted to get the machine gunner who hit him.

"We need to kill this guy," he urged his men. "We need to make sure he suffers in a very painful way."

Brasher was evacuated after the fight but learned later that he and his men had killed twenty Taliban fighters during the three-hour battle.

"Usually the guys you kill are the guys in charge because they are braver," Brasher said. "We had killed so many people in that spot they didn't have anybody else to go up against us."

For his gallantry, Army Major General Curtis M. Scarparrotti, commander of the 82nd Airborne Division, presented Brasher with a Silver Star, the Army's third-highest award for bravery, at a ceremony in October 2008.

"He was always out front exposing himself, making sure it was safe before he put his men in any danger," McGovern, Brasher's platoon leader during the battle, said in a TV interview. "He would rather get hit than any of his other guys."

Rehabilitating his arm has not been easy. Surgery allowed him to regain range of motion.

Brasher doesn't see his actions as heroic.

★★★

47

★★★

Major General Curtis M. Scaparrotti, commander of the 82nd Airborne Division, presents the Silver Star medal to Sergeant First Class James Brasher during a December 2007 ceremony at Fort Bragg, North Carolina. (Photo courtesy of James Brasher)

"When you ask most people who get awards, you are just doing your job, really," Brasher said. "So if that merits an award, I guess it does.

"The real honor is the guys that I was with seem to think I deserve that little bit of extra. They are the heroes. I am just the guy that shows them where to go." ★

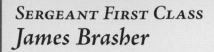

SERGEANT FIRST CLASS
James Brasher

U.S. Army

- Born September 19, 1979, in Albuquerque, New Mexico.

- Wife, Skye; no children.

- Joined Army in December 1998. Has been deployed twice to Iraq and twice to Afghanistan.

What he did

Repeatedly exposed himself to enemy fire while helping lead an assault on a village that was a Taliban stronghold, even after his arm had been shattered by a machine-gun burst.

Why he joined the Army

"To serve my country. It was always an option that I kept open the last few years in high school."

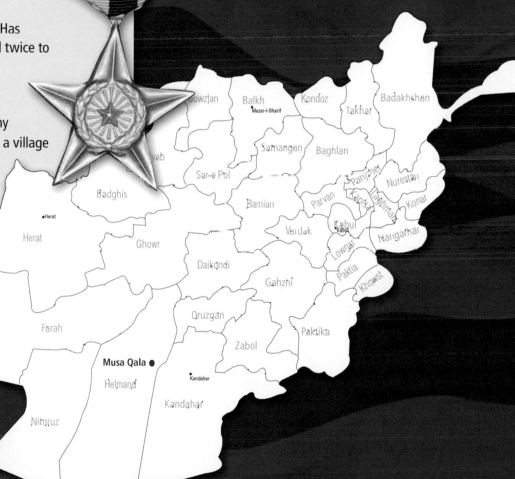

49

Michael D. Carter

U.S. Army, Silver Star

By Ashley Hamershock

SPECIALIST MICHAEL CARTER WASN'T SUPPOSED TO BE on that cliffside that day, April 6, 2008, taking intense fire from insurgents alongside U.S. Special Forces and native commandos in what is considered one of the legendary battles of the Afghanistan war.

The twenty-four-year-old combat cameraman was nearing the end of his twelve-month tour and thought he'd completed his last combat mission. Then his boss got pinkeye and asked Carter to fill in on the mission deep within Shok Valley, a well-known sanctuary of the Hezeb Islamic al Gulbadin terrorist organization.

Arriving with his gear, the Texas native got a hint of what was to come.

"The team just started stripping my whole kit apart, saying, 'You're not going to need this' because we were going just pretty much vertical. That's when I was like, 'Wow, OK.'"

Along with a dozen Green Berets and a small group of Afghan soldiers, Carter jumped from a hovering helicopter onto the remote, icy terrain of northeastern Afghanistan's Nuristan province. The team slogged through a frigid stream and scaled halfway up a cliff face toward its target village when insurgents suddenly started firing. Carter climbed to the next tier and scrambled over to join the detachment commander and combat controller.

The unit's interpreter was shot in the head not two feet away as he ran for cover at the outset of the fierce, seven-hour firefight. Insurgents had surrounded the American troops, who were far outnumbered, even with their Afghan commando allies.

"My bag got shot," Carter says. "It ripped through my camera and batteries and my Camelbak. I felt the Camelbak water running down my back. I thought I'd been shot. I was so pumped through with adrenaline. I thought, 'You gotta be kiddin' me.'"

He quickly realized it was water and got back to work, carrying a wounded team member out of the line of fire, then performing first aid and running back into immediate danger to recover the communication sergeant's radio.

Air support had been called in, and heavy debris rained down. Carter used his body to shield the seriously injured from further harm. Meanwhile, more nearby team members were shot.

Carter and another soldier left their nook to find another way

Specialist Michael Carter earned a Silver Star for his heroism on a sixty-foot, nearly vertical cliff in Afghanistan. He became the first U.S. combat cameraman to receive the military's third-highest decoration. (Photo courtesy of Michael Carter)

down the cliffs. They reported back to the commander that it wouldn't be easy.

"He was like, 'Will the guys live?' I was like, 'Yeah, they'll live.' He was like, 'All right, start taking them down.'"

Carter helped several wounded soldiers down the sixty-foot, nearly vertical face. When they couldn't climb any farther, Carter braced himself ten to fifteen feet below to catch them as they were dropped.

Seven hours later, they were back in the air. While many were injured, no American troops died that day. Two Afghan commandos were killed. Carter and nine others were awarded the Silver Star for their actions. He became the first U.S. combat cameraman to receive the military's third-highest decoration.

Asked what the citation means to him, he glanced down for a moment. "I'm honored."

The intense firefight and mounting injuries left no time for Carter to think about the worst-case scenario.

"I knew we were going to come out of it," he says. "I mean, I was with the Army's best. I'm just glad we all came out alive."

As it turns out, the cameraman never used his camera that day. It now sits in a museum in Fort Meade, Maryland.   ★

Specialist
Michael D. Carter

- Born September 26, 1983, in Smithville, Texas.

- Single

- Was deployed to Afghanistan from May 19, 2007, to May 4, 2008.

- Member of the 55th Signal Company (Combat Camera or COMCAM) based in Fort Meade, Maryland, assigned to Combined Joint Special Operations Task Force-Afghanistan (CJSOTF-A); now serves with the Joint POW/MIA Accounting Command.

What he did
Became the first combat cameraman to be awarded a Silver Star for heroism after helping his unit repel insurgents and escape a cliff-side ambush.

Why he joined the Army
"I've always wanted to. Both of my grandparents served. My mom's father was a Marine, is a Marine. My dad's father, he was in the Army, and I just wanted to."

Aaron Davis

U.S. Army, Silver Star

By Tim Holbert

SPECIALIST AARON DAVIS HAD SEEN COMBAT BEFORE during his fourteen-month tour, but nothing remotely like this. What started out as pop shots, well before daybreak, quickly grew into one of the deadliest and most controversial engagements of the war in Afghanistan.

And he would be in the heart of it.

In the days leading to the June 13, 2008, battle, Davis' forty-eight-man platoon from the 2nd Battalion, 503rd Infantry, 173rd Airborne Brigade Combat Team had begun construction of a patrol base near the village of Wanat in Konar province.

The region had become a hotbed of Taliban activity, a major supply line for insurgent fighters.

Davis' platoon was responsible for monitoring and disrupting their operations.

The unfinished patrol base consisted mainly of an area lightly surrounded by sandbags and barbed wire, and the American and a few dozen Afghan troops had little warning of the ambush.

"We knew it could happen," he said. "You expect the worst all the time; you need to be ready for anything to happen. But as far as intelligence goes, we weren't (alerted)."

Suddenly, two hundred Taliban surrounded the base, determined to run straight through them.

Davis, an anti-armor gunner, was in the TOW (tube-launched, optically tracked, wire-guided) truck. It was hit by a rocket-propelled grenade and caught fire.

With the truck destroyed, Davis was weaponless, and the platoon began taking serious casualties. Determined to help the men he called his brothers, Davis scrambled to find a weapon and began to return fire.

As the insurgents advanced, Davis was hit in the right leg with shrapnel from an exploding RPG. Ignoring the intense pain, he refused to leave the battlefield so he could help three severely injured soldiers until a medical evacuation team arrived. It saved their lives.

A humble Davis rejects any idea that his actions were heroic: "Well, I wasn't alone. We just moved as a team and got them out of there as soon as we could."

Soon, another RPG detonated nearby, its shrapnel cutting into Davis' left arm and right eye. Blinded by his own blood, Davis recalls praying before he felt the hand of a Marine, who pulled him to safety.

★★★
53
★★★

SPECIALST
Aaron Davis

U.S. Army

- Born in 1987 in Kilgore, Texas.

- Single.

- Joined the Army on Jan. 4, 2006, and deployed to Afghanistan on May 23, 2007, as an anti-armor gunner with 2nd Battalion, 503rd Infantry, 173rd Airborne Brigade Combat Team.

What he did

Wounded by shrapnel in his right leg, he refused to leave a remote Afghanistan battlefield, staying to provide aid to three severely injured comrades. Shrapnel from a later explosion injured him in the left arm and right eye.

Why he joined the Army

"I was a freshman in high school on 9/11. It hurt me to see people come here and do what they did, so afterwards I wanted to do my part."

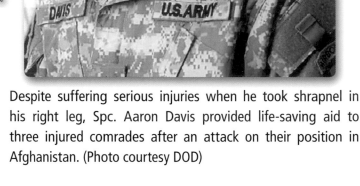

Despite suffering serious injuries when he took shrapnel in his right leg, Spc. Aaron Davis provided life-saving aid to three injured comrades after an attack on their position in Afghanistan. (Photo courtesy DOD)

Twenty-six others in his platoon were wounded, and nine, including their leader, First Lieutenant Jonathan Brostrom, were killed. The U.S. military estimated that twenty-one to fifty Taliban fighters were killed in the Battle of Wanat.

Today, Davis is back in the United States, recovering in his native Texas.

The battle also triggered self-examinations within the U.S. military to determine whether the unit was properly equipped and supported in the remote valley. It has led to three investigations, including one ordered in September by Gen. David Petraeus, head of the U.S. Central Command. ★

Lincoln V. Dockery

U.S. Army, Silver Star

By Peter Slavin

EXCEPT FOR THE INTELLIGENCE REPORT THAT AN IMPROvised explosive device had been planted in the area, November 16, 2007 appeared to be a normal day for the road-clearing platoon of the Army's 173rd Airborne Brigade in eastern Afghanistan.

The platoon's job as it set off down the Korengal Road was to find the IED. About an hour out, between the villages of Kandegal and Omar in Konar province, a detonation rocked the vehicle-mounted mine detector that had been leading the way.

Staff Sergeant Lincoln Dockery and other dismounted troops nearby were knocked down and dazed as more than 30 insurgents opened up from above with rocket-propelled grenades, machine guns and small arms.

Despite the heavy fire, Dockery was determined to get the driver out of the vehicle. He climbed up its side tire and beat repeatedly on the window until Private First Class Amador Magana, the driver, regained consciousness.

Unhurt, Magana gave him a thumbs-up sign, stood up and started firing his automatic weapon. Dockery decided

it was time to storm the enemy position about seventy-five feet above.

"It had to be done," Dockery recalled, noting that the remaining vehicles in the convoy were sitting ducks. "I guess all the training kicked in. I knew what had to be done without really thinking about it."

He and Specialist Corey Taylor rushed forward, then started inching upward on their bellies, throwing grenades and firing frequent rifle bursts. Three groups of insurgents — two on the mountain and one across the valley — saw them and lobbed gre-

Staff Sergeant Lincoln Dockery, wife Dominika and daughter Pria enjoy the festivities shortly after Dockery was awarded the Silver Star and Purple Heart medals in a ceremony on March 11, 2009, in Bamberg, Germany.

nades. Shrapnel hit Dockery in the right forearm, but he decided his injury wasn't major and pushed ahead.

He and Taylor fought their way up the mountainside and took cover at the base of a rock incline. Taliban fighters, lodged not far above them and firing down, were so close that Dockery could hear them talking.

Dockery finally managed to get his platoon leader, 1st Lieutenant William Cromie, on the radio and asked for help. Cromie, fighting off the attack from below with the rest of the unit, couldn't see where Dockery and Taylor were or determine when other troops could reach them.

Minutes went by. The two soldiers were running out of ammunition, and the enemy knew where they were. What if the Taliban rushed them?

Cromie decided to go up the mountain himself, carrying extra ammunition, and trio began pushing the fighters back from the rock and toward their compound.

Finally, Cromie hurled their last grenade into the enemy compound, and Dockery and Taylor rushed toward it. Dockery, now out of M-14 ammunition, relied on his pistol for the rest of the fight as the insurgents retreated.

Cromie ran back down the mountain, returning with six soldiers, and the team made a room-by-room search of the building. There were no bodies in the compound, but Dockery is certain that the enemy suffered casualties, judging by "the amount of blood that we saw."

They also found the wire and parts used to make the IED.

Cromie, who also received a Silver Star, said in interviews that he didn't want to think about what would have happened had Dockery not been present.

Staff Sergeant Lincoln Dockery takes a break from route-clearance operations in Konar province, Afghanistan, in 2008.

While every military school teaches the bold tactics Dockery took to repel the attackers, Cromie noted, "If asked to charge into an enemy, uphill and within hand-grenade range, most people know 'yes' only as a book answer." ★

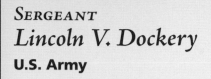

SERGEANT
Lincoln V. Dockery
U.S. Army

- Born May 13, 1983, in Runnemede, New Jersey, now lives in Bamberg, Germany.

- Wife, Dominika; children, Lincoln, five, and Pria, two.

- Joined the Army in August 2001, deployed to Afghanistan in May 2007. Also has served tours of duty in Kosovo and Iraq.

What he did
Led another soldier up a rock incline and stormed the position of enemy fighters who had attacked his road-clearing patrol.

Why he joined the Army
"I joined because both my brothers are older than me and they both went to college. They were still living at home, and I just didn't want to be like them. So at the time the only way to get out of the house was to join the Army. . . . I just didn't want to be at home no more."

Steve M. Egoavil

U.S. Army, Soldier's Medal

By S.L. Alligood

PRIVATE FIRST CLASS STEVE EGOAVIL stops his search through the rubble of the bombed mess hall.

Did he hear something? He listens again.

Another soldier hears it, too.

The voice is faint and desperate: "I'm here. I'm here. Help me."

Beneath the rubble, coated in dust, an unknown soldier is trapped, his foot beneath a toppled rock pillar. A half-hour earlier the pinned soldier was eating supper with two friends when a bomb-laden vehicle stopped outside the building at Sabari, a forward operating base in the Khost province of southeastern Afghanistan.

About that time, Egoavil and fellow soldiers from the Fifth Battalion of the 101st Aviation Combat Brigade were finishing a fast roping exercise, rappelling from a hovering helicopter.

For two months since members of the unit had deployed from Fort Campbell, Kentucky, they had continued to train at Forward Operating Base Camp Salerno. Egoavil and his buddies wondered if they would ever get a mission.

That day, March 3, 2007, it would come at Sabari, a twenty-minute chopper ride away.

"Our faces changed completely from having fun doing the fast roping exercise to everyone jumping in the vehicle to go back to the arms room to get our equipment and get suited up," recalls Egoavil, then twenty-five.

Dusk settled in as three Black Hawks took off for Sabari. Upon landing, the unit's medic called for Egoavil, who also had received training as a medic.

PRIVATE FIRST CLASS
Steve M. Egoavil
U.S. Army

- Born August 23, 1983 in Torrance, California
- Joined the Army on May 10, 2006. Deployed to Afghanistan on January 12, 2007.
- Now a specialist, was a private first class at the time of the incident, when he was assigned to Pathfinders, Fifth Battalion of the 101st Aviation Combat Brigade.

What he did
Rescued a fellow soldier who was trapped under a concrete pillar while a crane held the swaying ceiling of the building over him.

Why he joined the Army
"I joined the military to make a difference. How I lived my life and how I had gone day to day, I felt I could be something more. Making money and living day to day for myself just kind of seemed to be a waste. I felt that if I joined the military I'd have good training, have the opportunity to make a difference in this world."

In the devastated mess hall, bodies were everywhere. Everyone fervently pulled rubble away, Egoavil remembers: "Everyone was so frantic at it."

That's when he heard the pinned soldier's faint, plaintive cry. Using the lights from a forklift to illuminate the surreal scene, Egoavil and others began widening a hole to pull the soldier out.

But the toppled pillar proved too heavy. They rushed to get jacks from several Humvees. Wedging broken two-by-fours under the jacks inched the pillar off the soldier's leg.

Egoavil, five-foot-three and 150 pounds with his combat boots on, surveyed the hole in the rubble the men had cleared. He could squeeze through, he told his platoon sergeant, if he took off his body armor.

"I didn't hear any 'No's,' so I did it and went in," Egoavil says.

After wriggling into the rubble, he pivoted the injured soldier 180 degrees so outside rescuers could pull him out by his shoulders instead of his injured leg. All the while, a crane held the swaying ceiling of the building aloft.

"That was probably the scariest part right there because the ceiling was swinging over my head," Egoavil says. "Oh, this is not good. But I didn't even think of that until after the fact."

Egoavil never learned the name of the man he saved. When they exited the small rescue hole, both men were covered in dust.

"I mean everything was covered, even his name tapes," he says. "At the time I didn't even think to ask. The whole thing was to get him out and look for others."

Rescuers worked through the rubble for more than two hours. Unfortunately, the injured soldier's two friends from the 82nd Airborne Division did not survive the blast. Their bodies were found in another fallen section.

And the soldier Egoavil saved?

He's not sure, "but from what they've told me . . . he did all right."

To Egoavil, the actions that earned him a Soldier's Medal for saving the life of another solder weren't that special.

Not for a soldier.

"That's what we do," he says. "That's what we're trained for. I knew had that happened to me, I knew a soldier, given the opportunity, would save my life." ★

(Photo courtesy of Steve Egoavil)

Michael Espejo stands watch at Torkham Gate on the Afghanistan-Pakistan border on August 24, 2007. Espejo and his fellow soldiers from the 66th Military Police Company accepted an invitation from the Afghan Border Police to participate in the Afghan Independence Day festivities at the gate.

★★★
60
★★★

Michael A. Espejo Jr.

U.S. Army, Silver Star

By Thomas L. Day

Tʜᴇ Aʀᴍʏ ᴜɴɪᴛ ᴡᴀs ᴏɴ ᴘᴀᴛʀᴏʟ ɪɴ ᴛʜᴇ Bᴀᴛɪ Kᴏᴛ district east of Jalalabad, Afghanistan, when it came upon the burning vehicle's shell. On the side of the road, lying face up on the ground, was a man in an Afghan police uniform, apparently wounded.

Sergeant Michael Espejo rushed to pull him away from the wreckage.

"I picked him off the ground," Espejo recalled. "As I was taking this individual, I had his left arm draped over my shoulders and my right arm around his back, kind of holding his chest as I was carrying him away."

Suddenly, the man regained consciousness.

"I started feeling his chest with my fingers, and it was bulky and hard," Espejo said. "I looked down at his chest and it looked like what appeared to be a ballistic vest.

"I looked at his arms, his left arm that was draped over my shoulders, and I saw that he had a wire running out from his sleeves into his palms and kind of a light switch device."

This was no fallen comrade. It was a suicide bomber.

Espejo quickly threw the man to the ground and warned his team leader, approaching with a first aid bag, to stay away.

Using Pashto phrases he had learned, Espejo screamed at the man to sit down and raise his hands. Espejo backed away, keeping his M4 rifle pointed at the suicide bomber.

It became clear the man didn't intend to leave the engagement alive.

"I saw that after multiple warnings, he was trying to hit the switch," Espejo said, "and that's when I decided to neutralize him."

Espejo's actions saved the lives of four other soldiers, two State Department officials and a gathering crowd of civilian onlookers, according to the citation accompanying his Silver Star, the third-highest commendation for bravery. He had exhausted all other options before he killed the suicide bomber, the Army said.

Some details about the September 27, 2007, ambush-in-the-making were still unclear. Why was the suicide bomber on

Sergeant Michael Espejo receives his Silver Star medal from Lieutenant General Charles H. Jacoby Jr., commanding general of I Corps and Fort Lewis, as Major Frank Grippe, I Corps command sergeant major, and Espejo's wife Rosa watch.

his back before Espejo's team arrived? What happened to the burning vehicle, apparently the result of a car bomb that had detonated?

Espejo said his patrol had received reports that insurgents in the area were donning official uniforms. It seemed likely that the vehicle bomb had exploded prematurely, knocking aside the bomber.

"Or they just could have been setting the whole thing up," Espejo said. "I don't know, to tell you the truth." ★

Sergeant Michael Espejo was profiled in an Army ad that detailed his quick thinking in Afghanistan.

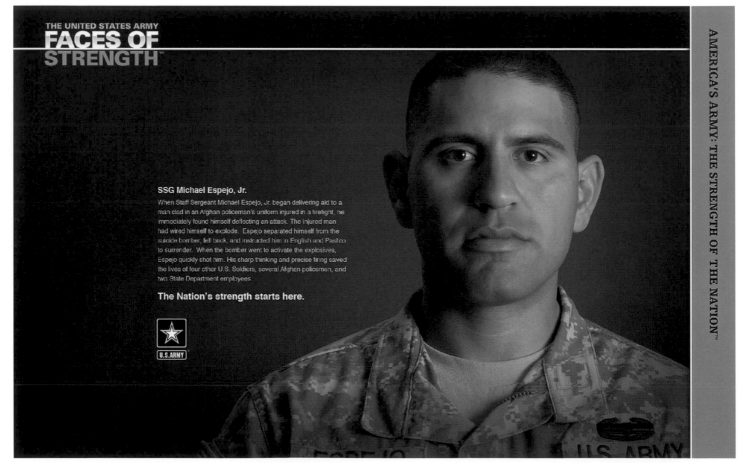

Sergeant
Michael Espejo Jr.

U.S. Army

- Born May 29, 1982, in Indio, California, but considers Bakersfield, California, his home.

- Wife, Rosa; children, Sander and Madison.

- Joined the Marines at age nineteen, attended college after finishing his enlistment, then re-enlisted for six years in 2005, this time as a military policeman in the Army. Has served two tours of duty in Afghanistan.

- At the time of the incident was a sergeant with the 1st Squad, 1st Platoon, 66th Military Police Company, 42nd Military Police Brigade, from Fort Lewis, Wash. Later promoted to staff sergeant.

- Is a member of the Sergeant Audie Murphy Club, a society that admits members based on performance in front of a board, quizzing applicants on the minutiae of Army regulations.

What he did

Single-handedly stopped a suicide bomber disguised as an Afghan national police officer.

Why he joined the military

"I wanted to serve my country."

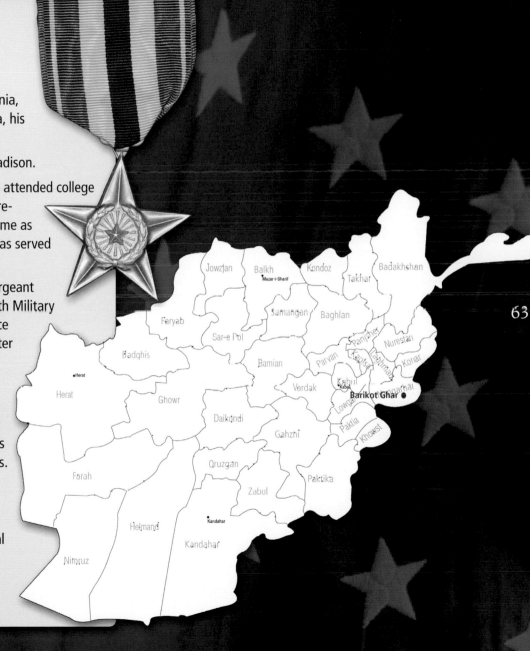

David R. Hutchinson

U.S. Army Reserve, Silver Star

By Thomas L. Day

PRIVATE FIRST CLASS DAVID HUTCHINSON WAS ONLY four days into a twelve-month deployment with the 420th Engineer Brigade in eastern Afghanistan and was riding on his first patrol to get acquainted with the surroundings in Paktika province.

On the morning of May 21, 2008 Hutchinson, then twenty-one, was in the third of four trucks on what was supposed to be a three and a half- to four-hour convoy.

"About halfway through the country," he said, "we got ambushed."

The convoy had entered a funnel point in a wall, "just long enough to get all four trucks in there," Hutchinson said. It was the perfect spot for an ambush, and the convoy drew fire from high ground in two directions.

When all four trucks were maneuvered into the target, about two dozen Taliban fighters opened fire with AK-47s, sniper rifles, machine guns and rocket-propelled grenades.

"I saw like fifteen or twenty guys pop up on my right," Hutchinson said.

He started firing the MK-19 grenade launcher mounted on his truck. The "Mark 19" can fire up to sixty rounds a minute. Hutchinson would need every round.

"About as fast I could shoot," Hutchinson said, "that's how fast they were popping up."

All seventeen soldiers in the convoy fired back, and Hutchinson used an MK-19 to destroy a Taliban machine gun nest. The attackers immediately redirected their fire at the third vehicle, and Hutchinson's gun turret would leave the engagement with more than one hundred bullet marks.

When the Taliban launched rocket-propelled grenades, the first and second hit Hutchinson's vehicle squarely.

"It knocked me out of my turret and laid me out flat in the cabin," Hutchinson said. "I was numb from my waist down at first, for the first couple of minutes."

The RPGs convinced the convoy commander that the Taliban attack had

Hutchinson is shown in training at Fort McCoy, Wisconsin, before being deployed to Afghanistan in 2008. (Photo courtesy of David Hutchinson)

fire superiority, so the drivers of all four vehicles stood on their gas pedals. Several kilometers down the road — out of harm's way — they stopped to treat casualties.

Hutchinson didn't have the luxury of waiting that long. First Sergeant David Gussberry was bleeding heavily and needed immediate first aid.

"He took shrapnel to the face and his arms and the side of his chest," Hutchinson recalled. "His entire upper body was covered in blood."

Despite his own wounds, Hutchinson rolled over and stanched Gussberry's wounds with his own first aid kit. And when a Medevac helicopter arrived with only a single litter, Hutchinson insisted that Gussberry be evacuated first.

Two F-15s escorted the rest of the convoy back to the nearest base. All 17 soldiers survived the attack.

Hutchinson's deployment was a short one; he was sent home the day after the firefight. On June 6, 2009, the 65th anniversary of D-Day, Hutchinson became the fifth Army Reserve soldier to be awarded the Silver Star. ★

★★★
66
★★★

(Photo courtesy of David Hutchinson)

Private First Class
David R. Hutchinson
U.S. Army Reserve

- Born April 3, 1987, in Humble, Texas.

- Was married on July 18, 2009.

- Was a private first class at the time of the incident.

- Has two cousins who were also in the Army.

What he did
Knocked out a Taliban machine-gun nest when his convoy was ambushed. After he was hurt when his truck was hit with enemy rocket-propelled grenades, he helped stop the bleeding of an injured comrade.

Why he joined the Army
"A lot of the male figures on my mother's side of the family have served in some capacity or other. Most of them were Air Force. I'm not a fan of flying too much. So I joined the Army . . . and then to pay for school as well."

Sean R. Laycox

**Nevada Army National Guard,
Distinguished Flying Cross**

By Keith A. Rogers

A S ITS REAR WHEELS TOUCHED THE GROUND, BULLETS ripped through the Chinook helicopter. Army door gunners on both sides responded with their M-60 machine guns while nearby explosions from rockets fired by escorting Apache AH-64 gun ships above rocked the Chinook.

Engulfed in the fury, Chief Warrant Officer Sean Laycox was determined to land his Chinook and insert Special Forces soldiers near a village where several high-value Taliban leaders were meeting.

A relatively peaceful twenty-one years in the Army and Guard was changing abruptly on April 18, 2005, as Laycox made his first air assault into the teeth of the enemy. It would not be his last treacherous landing that day.

What had started as a monotonous tour for him —delivering supplies for Operation Enduring Freedom — was turning into a violent battle at Deh Chopan, in remote southeastern Afghanistan.

As Laycox led another Chinook and the Apaches to the landing zone along-

(Photo by Gary Thompson/*Las Vegas Review-Journal*)

side an orchard, the insurgents emerged from a row of mud buildings.

The second Chinook touched down while Laycox circled back to land. In a hail of bullets, he said, "We were basically sitting ducks there."

While Special Forces soldiers scrambled out the back ramp, Laycox radioed for the Apaches to provide cover.

"You could hear the Apaches shooting their rockets to the mud wall off to the right, which was very distracting," he said. "During this whole time there was a huge explosion to the aircraft, the six o'clock position."

Laycox initially thought it was from an Apache-fired rocket. He later learned that an insurgent had rushed the aircraft with a hand grenade. Special Forces soldiers shot him before he could reach the helicopter.

"He dropped the hand grenade, and that's what the explosion was we heard," Laycox said. "Fortunately for us, he didn't get it on board."

His bullet-riddled helicopter had taken a couple in the front transmission, and Laycox saw that the Chinook was about fifty degrees hotter than usual — dangerously close to its limit.

"As soon as we got those guys off, we took off as quickly as we could and kind of accelerated low-level so we could get behind the hill where they couldn't shoot at us any more," he said.

Into view came the sister Chinook, also shot up and leaking oil.

"So we found a spot for him to land in a little valley, kind of a depression where we could hide the helicopter the best we could," Laycox said. "He landed there, and we landed behind him."

The battle raging, word soon came to remove both Special Forces teams. But only Laycox's Chinook was still operable.

He flew back to the battle, again drawing fire on approach and in the landing zone. Mortars and rocket-propelled grenades pounded the area as the Chinook was loaded.

It seemed like an eternity for the troops to load, Laycox said. Thirty seconds turned into minutes as he kept thinking: "You can't leave them there. Once you leave them there, they're sitting ducks themselves."

So the Chinook crew waited. "They're (Special Forces) doing their best to get everyone on board," he said. "But time stands still for the air crew. . . . This is what we have to do. . . . It's part of the job. There's an obligation to the soldiers that you put in."

The Chinook sat on the ground for five or six minutes. "The whole time we could hear these explosions, and you could see them once in a while. They loaded up all the dead Taliban and troops and then we got out of there."

Later, he and his crew went back a third time to retrieve the crew from the stranded Chinook.

Laycox received the Distinguished Flying Cross, and two Air Medals for valor in other engagements in September 2005 from Vice President Dick Cheney in a hangar at Bagram Air Base.

The citation reflected the real bottom line: no U.S. soldiers were killed.

In part, it read: "The skillful piloting and selfless decisions of . . . Laycox throughout the battle and his valorous determination to support the inserted assault force had no doubt saved the lives of many on this day." ★

CHIEF WARRANT OFFICER
Sean R. Laycox
Army National Guard

- Born June 10, 1959, in San Francisco, California.

- Married to Jas, with two children, Mitchell, eighteen, and Caitlin, fourteen.

- Nickname is "Mr. Pickles."

- Served with Delta Company, 113th Aviation, on a peace-keeping tour in Bosnia in 2002 and 2003, and with the Nevada Army National Guard in Operation Enduring Freedom in 2005 and 2006.

What he did
Piloted his Chinook helicopter into a battle zone, dropping off U.S. soldiers and repeatedly returning amid heavy enemy fire to pick up the dead and wounded, and stranded survivors.

Why he joined the National Guard
"When I was growing up I just had a lot of uncles who were former military, so I was kind of surrounded by that. My dad had been in the Army, so I always had a love of aviation."

Jowzjan
Balkh
  Mazar-i-Sharif
Kondoz
Takhar
Badakhshan

Faryab
Samangan
Baghlan

Sar-e Pol
Badghis
Bamian
Parvan
Panjsher
Nurestan
Kapisa
Laghman
Konar

Herat
  Herat
Ghowr
Vardak
Kabul
  Kabul
Nangarhar

Daikondi
Lowgar
Paktia
Khowst

Gahzni

Oruzgan
Deh Chopan
Paktika

Farah
Zabol

Helmand
  Kandahar

Nimruz
Kandahar

69

(Laycox photo by Gary Thompson/*Las Vegas Review-Journal*)

(Photo by Guy Calaf)

Jamyn A. Peterson

U.S. Army Reserve, Bronze Star with Valor

By Wesley Millett

THE FIRST HE SAW OF THE ENEMY WERE THE MUZZLE flashes.

More than a hundred insurgents were peppering the Humvee ahead of Staff Sergeant Jamyn Peterson as soldiers spilled out of the disabled truck and staggered around in a daze. The turret gunner had been hit, mortally wounded by an 82mm shell that plowed into the truck from only thirty yards away.

The convoy — five Humvees and several Afghan police trucks — was headed back from a combat mission in the mountains of southern Afghanistan on June 16, 2007, when the lead truck suddenly came under attack and crashed into a boulder.

His Humvee pulled up behind the truck and was soon under fire itself, Peterson recalled: "The bullets were pinging and popping off the armor."

Peterson had up-armored the Humvee but had little time to take pride in the fact that the rocket-propelled grenades fired at it were glancing off the steel plating.

His crew needed to rescue the gunner and get the wounded soldiers into Peterson's Humvee, but that would require covering fire.

"I knew that I had to leave the truck and set up my M240," he said. "If I didn't get out, they were going to die. I was also convinced that if I did get out, I was going to die. I was pretty much resigned to that possibility."

Peterson was shot through the thigh as he exited the Humvee. He hobbled across to the disabled vehicle and set up the M240 machine gun on the hood of the truck. He had two thousand rounds linked to his belt

Holding the trigger down, he fired the gun until the barrel was melting and he was out of ammunition. Peterson soon came under heavy fire, and as he leaned on the hood, an RPG bore through a tire and into the engine block beneath him.

Badakhshan

Takhar

lan

Panjsher   Nurestan

Kapisa Laghman
Konar

Kabul

Kabul   Nangarhar

Lowgar

Paktia   Khowst

1310 01 159 6043 6342
48 CARTRIDGES 40MM
M430 HEDP LINKED
W/M16A2 LINKS

(Photo courtesy of Jamyn Peterson)

(Photo courtesy of Jamyn Peterson)

"For some very fortunate reason," Peterson said, "it never blew."

Another soldier took his position, allowing Peterson to direct his attention to the wounded and removing sensitive weapons and equipment from the disabled truck.

"We managed to get the turret gunner on a stretcher, but he knew he wasn't going to make it." Peterson said. "He wanted to know who was on his gun, and he asked that a message be given to his family."

He was soon evacuated, and the soldiers from the disabled truck were loaded into Peterson's Humvee. "It was meant to hold five soldiers, so we were in pretty close quarters with ten men . . . plus a bomb dog."

Meanwhile, air support from French F15s had been called in, and the insurgents came under a devastating attack.

"You can imagine what it was like with bombs exploding 90 feet away, dirt being thrown up everywhere and the ground shaking," Peterson related with some amusement. "We got out of there as soon as we could."

Peterson downplayed his injury and the lives he saved.

"I had set up a medical clinic in the village where my unit was deployed and learned how to treat certain wounds," he said. "The bullet went through my thigh, so I was able to clean and bandage the gunshot myself.

"Whatever I may have done, credit belongs to the Afghan police as well. When the rest of the convoy reached us, the Afghans pulled ahead of the disabled Humvee in their unarmored truck. They got hit hard, and two were killed. They definitely helped buy us time to remove our men from the kill zone."

★

STAFF SERGEANT
Jamyn A. Peterson
U.S. Army Reserve

- Born March 3, 1977, in New Richmond, Wisconsin, where he still lives.

- Married to Elizabeth.

- Joined the Army on December 12, 1994. Deployed to Iraq from February to October 2003 and to Afghanistan from December 2007 to March 2008.

- Was assigned as a Team Leader for Psychological Operations to A Company, 13th Psychological Operations Battalion, in direct support of Combined Joint Special Operations Task Force-Afghanistan at Firebase Anaconda, Oruzgan province.

What he did
Although shot through the thigh, he provided covering fire and evacuated soldiers wounded in an attack on his convoy.

Why he joined the Army
"The reason I joined was because of what had happened in Somalia in 1993. I saw our soldiers being dragged through the streets, and it got me all fired up."

Jamyn Peterson, third from right, meets with members of the Taliban, with whom he regularly discussed minimizing attacks on U.S. soldiers, especially with improvised explosive devices. (Photo courtesy of Jamyn Peterson)

73

(Photo courtesy of Mark Radwich)

Mark A. Radwich

U.S. Air Force, Army Commendation Medal and Air Force Combat Action Medal

By Tom Lindley

FIRST CAME THE CHATTER ON THE RADIO: KEEP AN EYE on a suspicious Toyota parked on the opposite side of the road.

Seconds later came the explosion, followed by a fireball.

Staff Sergeant Mark Radwich, a U.S. Air Force medic attached to the 203rd Army Unit, couldn't see what had gone wrong two vehicles ahead. He was encased in combat armor in the back seat of a Humvee, an M-4 assault rifle between his legs and an Afghan scarf covering his face to fight off the dust.

So he never saw the Toyota shoot across the road and take aim on the lead Humvee in Radwich's four-vehicle convoy. The soldiers were returning to Camp Clark, their forward operating base, after picking up supplies about six miles away at Camp Salerno in Khost, Afghanistan.

The Humvee's driver swerved but not in time to avoid the blast triggered by the suicide vehicle.

"We couldn't even see the first two vehicles in convoy," Radwich said of the ambush on August 13, 2007. "The radios went out except in our vehicle. Nobody could really hear what was going on outside. So we stopped."

Procedure called for first checking the area for explosives or other forms of attack, but Radwich was in a hurry to grab his medical bag.

"I was preparing and basically telling them I got to go," Radwich said. "They finally gave me permission."

Once outside, all Radwich could see was smoke as he and another medic jogged to the spot where the first vehicle had careened down a fifteen-foot embankment into the riverbed. About fifty meters of open terrain separated them from the Humvee.

"Take it nice and easy," the Army medic, a combat veteran, said, putting his hand on Radwich's shoulder. But as they reached the edge of the embankment, someone yelled, "Incoming fire."

"We heard some rounds go up over our heads, and a light jog turned into a very, very fast run," Radwich said.

At the bottom, three soldiers in the Humvee already were out of the vehicle in a defensive position, firing rounds at

★ ★ ★
75
★ ★ ★

insurgents who wanted to clean up what the suicide bomber had left unfinished.

In the middle of the firefight, Radwich helped treat the gunner from the blasted vehicle who had suffered burns to his face and was in shock. He treated a second soldier for a concussion and an injured ankle.

Radwich also got off some rounds of his own and later helped hold an insurgent hostage after the shooting stopped.

Radwich says his unit's training and teamwork led to surviving the ambush. That training also brought out something else in him — a sense of duty.

"I needed to go help. I wanted to help," Radwich said. "I needed to figure out what hap-

pened. There were two guys that I was with. . . . I just needed to get my eyes on them and make sure they were OK."

It wasn't until it was all over that Radwich could hear his heart pounding in his ears.

Radwich terms the event "very, very small" in the grand scheme of things, saving his praise for members of the 203rd.

"At the very end (of his tour of duty), we lost a significant amount of people in such a very, very short time. I wish I could say that it was all good, but those parts at the end were not good." ★

STAFF SERGEANT
Mark A. Radwich
U.S. Air Force

* Born August 7, 1980, in Lawrence, Massachusetts.

* Wife Meghan; two children.

* Joined the Air Force on January 5, 2000; deployed to Afghanistan on July 27, 2007. Served on a Brigade Support Team attached to the 203rd Army Unit in Khost, Afghanistan, where he was the noncommissioned officer in charge of the Troop Medical Clinic at Camp Clark. Served three tours of duty overseas, one each to Afghanistan, Oman and Kurdistan.

What he did
Under fire in the midst of an attack on his convoy, he treated two comrades injured by a roadside car bomb.

Why he joined the Air Force
"I very much wanted to join the military somehow since I was a kid."

(Photo courtesy of Mark Radwich)

Sarun Sar

U.S. Army, Silver Star

By Kevin Maurer

H E WAS NO STRANGER TO WAR. Sarun Sar's first combat experience came in his native Cambodia, where he fought with anti-Vietnamese guerrillas. But when the Vietnamese invaded, his family was split up. His father died in prison, his brother was executed for smuggling weapons for anti-government guerrillas and his mother and two other brothers died from starvation.

Sar ended up on the western side of the country, where he was wounded several times and eventually sent to a refugee camp in Thailand.

★★★
78
★★★

There, he met up with his older sister and eventually moved to the United States. Sar gained his citizenship while in the Army and deployed all over the world with Special Forces to places such as Bosnia, Kosovo, Africa, Colombia and Afghanistan.

In the latter country, he would distinguish himself again.

On March 5, 2005, Sar could see the Taliban fighters running from the village as his Black Hawk helicopter touched down.

"Follow me," Sar screamed to his 7th Special Forces Group teammates before jumping to the ground, hoping to cut the enemy off.

He could hear radio reports about the team's other helicopter taking fire as he rushed up the snowy mountain in Paktika province along the Pakistan border. He saw several Taliban running toward some woods. Another ran into a house.

Sar reached the house, throwing himself against a wall near the door and waiting for the rest of his team.

But "I didn't feel anyone tap me on the shoulder," said Sar, who was the Special Forces team sergeant, the most senior enlisted soldier.

Looking back down the hill, he saw that his teammates were pinned down by enemy fire. It was just Sar and a medic trapped at the house, far from their unit.

The squat house was made of thick mud and rock with a small door cut out. As Sar peeked inside, thick smoke hung inside the room. He barreled through the small, low opening, gun at the ready, and was halfway in when the flashlight on his M4 rifle illuminated the face of a Taliban fighter.

The enemy's muzzle flash lit up the darkness — three times.

Two shots missed. But the third hit the edge of Sar's Kevlar helmet at his forehead, the force throwing him back out the door.

"I will never forget that little flash I saw," Sar said. "He was waiting. It felt like I was hit in the head with a hammer."

Dazed, he rolled back outside and started screaming, "I'm hit! I'm hit!" to the medic. The medic searched for a wound, but the bullet hadn't penetrated Sar's helmet. Sar pulled a flash-bang stun grenade and threw it into the room before he re-entered the house and killed the Taliban fighter.

Kunduz
Takhar
Badakhshan
angan
Baghlan
Panjsher
Nuristan
Parwan
Kapisa
Laghman
Kunar
Wardak
Kabul
Logar
Nangarhar
nzni
Paktya
Khost
Paktika
Paktika

His charge up the mountain had disrupted the Taliban ambush and prevented his team from getting bogged down.

Major John Litchfield, the Special Forces team leader at the time, said Sar's actions also inspired the team to push up the hill.

"The rest of the team was under fire and pretty well pinned down," Litchfield said. "Human nature takes over, and you start clawing for a piece of ground. Sar did the opposite of that. We certainly wouldn't have achieved the goal in the same manner, and some of us could have been severely wounded."

Soon afterward, the Special Forces team cleared the other huts in the village and rounded up a huge cache of enemy weapons, including rocket-propelled grenades, bomb-making materials and explosives. Sar and another soldier were the only wounded Americans.

Looking back to the time on that mountain in 2005, Sar said he wouldn't change what he did:

"That is how we do things. I would still go in the house. Next time, the whole team would follow behind me." ★

SERGEANT
Sarun Sar
U.S. Army

* Born May 15, 1966, in Phnom Penh, Cambodia.

* Married; one daughter.

• Joined the Army in January 1985, deployed to Afghanistan in October 2004. Was promoted to sergeant major. Had two tours of duty to Afghanistan and numerous tours throughout the Pacific theater.

What he did
Disrupted a Taliban ambush that had pinned down his unit and led a charge that eventually uncovered a large cache of enemy weapons.

Why he joined the Army
"I just wanted to serve my country. I only planned to do three years. I guess it (the Army) just grew on me."

Randy A. Shorter
U.S. Army, Silver Star
Gregory A. Waters
U.S. Army, Silver Star

By Thomas L. Day

THE IMPACT FROM THE BOMB SENT SPECIALIST Gregory Waters bouncing around the armored vehicle like a rattle, knocking off his Kevlar helmet and leaving him and two others unconscious. Their sergeant's nose and one arm were broken.

Their Mine Resistant Ambush Protected vehicle had been leading three others in a convoy from the 506th Infantry Regiment on July 30, 2008. They had stopped about fifteen kilometers from their base near Ghazni, a Taliban stronghold in eastern Afghanistan, on their way home from an uneventful overnight patrol of a supply bridge.

Now, after being rocked by improvised explosive devices, more than two dozen Taliban fighters opened fire with small arms and rocket-propelled grenades from about nine hundred meters away.

Sergeant First Class Randy Shorter was riding in the last MRAP when he noticed that all the fire was focused on the lead vehicle.

"Their primary focus was just trying to kill everyone around that MRAP," Shorter said of the insurgents.

He grabbed an AT4 rocket launcher — a shoulder-fired device with barely enough range to reach the attackers — and fired it to buy some time. Remaining soldiers in the convoy jumped from their vehicles to return fire with their .50-caliber machine guns and M4 rifles.

Shorter then ran toward the lead vehicle, hoping someone was still alive inside it.

Waters had begun to regain consciousness. When he opened his eyes, he saw Private First Class Frank Whorton pinned to the floor by an eighty-four-pound, .50-caliber machine gun. But Whorton and Specialist Paul Wind were still alive. Waters could hear their sergeant, Porter Charles, screaming in pain and tried to grab a radio to tell others that he and the crew were still alive.

But the radios were dead.

Under heavy fire, Shorter reached the lead vehicle and opened the rear door. Waters was first out, stumbling to a spot fifty meters on the opposite side of the road from the Taliban attackers.

Shorter grabbed Whorton and carried him on his shoulders away from the vehicle. When Shorter went back for Charles and Wind, Waters was on his feet and ready to help. He removed Wind from the vehicle and out of the line of fire.

"There really wasn't much cover," Waters said. "We were trying to hide behind the damaged vehicle and use that for cover."

Once clear, Waters was left to treat the other three. Meanwhile, Shorter called in an air strike.

Two A10 Thunderbolts were five minutes away, however, and the convoy's ammunition was dwindling.

"One of the .50-caliber machine guns overheated due to the large volume of fire that we had to put on the enemy, just to keep them at bay," Shorter recalled. And two M240 machine guns were out of ammo.

As the A10s approached, the ground moved — and so did the Taliban attackers, bounding forward, knowing the pilots would be reluctant to fire near the American line.

They didn't move quickly enough.

Shorter sent a smoke grenade toward the Taliban line, showing the pilots where to fire. The pilots circled, unsure of the exact location and firing several smoke rounds of their own. Finally, over the radio, Shorter and the pilots calibrated the exact target.

The A10s unloaded, firing about ten missiles at the Taliban position.

Forty-five minutes after the roadside bomb detonated, the first Medevac helicopter arrived and loaded Charles, Whorton and Wind. Waters stayed behind, not wanting to leave the unit without a medic as the gunfire continued.

Finally, the A10s finished off the remaining Taliban.

An estimated thirty insurgents had been killed. And except for the four Americans injured in the lead vehicle, no other U.S. soldiers were injured in the attack.

Waters is unable to offer specifics about his treatment or recovery, unaware even of the number of stitches in his head: "I think we glued it back together. To be honest with you, sir, the following week and a half after that is really kind of a blur."

Clearheaded or not, he was back on duty just a couple of days later. ★

Sergeant First Class
Randy A. Shorter
U.S. Army

- Born November 9, 1977, in Makati City, Philippines, but considers Anaheim, California, his home.
- Wife, Sheryll; daughters, Maylanie, thirteen, and Ariana, nine.
- Joined the Army on October 15, 1996, and has served two tours of duty in Iraq and one in Afghanistan.

What he did
Helped rescue four soldiers under heavy fire after their patrol vehicle was hit by a roadside bomb, then called in and helped coordinate an air strike to wipe out the Taliban attackers.

Why he joined the Army
He became a father at a young age and said he was having difficulty supporting his family. "I wanted to give them a better life."

Randy Shorter's quick reactions after an insurgent's bomb hit near his convoy averted a potential disaster for U.S. troops. No U.S. soldiers died in the incident, and approximately thirty insurgents were killed. (Photo courtesy of Randy Shorter)

★★★
83
★★★

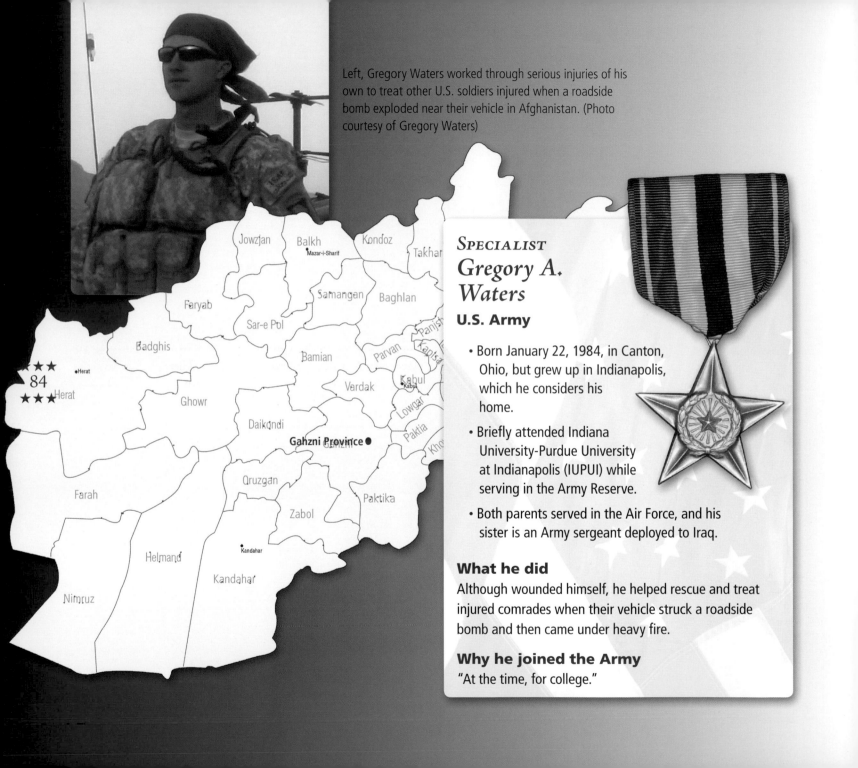

Left, Gregory Waters worked through serious injuries of his own to treat other U.S. soldiers injured when a roadside bomb exploded near their vehicle in Afghanistan. (Photo courtesy of Gregory Waters)

SPECIALIST
Gregory A. Waters
U.S. Army

- Born January 22, 1984, in Canton, Ohio, but grew up in Indianapolis, which he considers his home.

- Briefly attended Indiana University-Purdue University at Indianapolis (IUPUI) while serving in the Army Reserve.

- Both parents served in the Air Force, and his sister is an Army sergeant deployed to Iraq.

What he did
Although wounded himself, he helped rescue and treat injured comrades when their vehicle struck a roadside bomb and then came under heavy fire.

Why he joined the Army
"At the time, for college."

Marc Silvestri

U.S. Army, Bronze Star With Valor

By Brian Mockenhaupt

MARC SILVESTRI SQUEEZED BEHIND A ROCK AND watched a bullet smack the dirt where his foot had just been. Rounds zipped overhead. His patrol, spread out halfway up a mountain in Afghanistan on August 24, 2008, was under fire from three sides.

"They had the high ground," Silvestri says. "They started coming at us from the right of us, above us and the left of us."

He looked back down the mountainside and saw his platoon leader, First Lieutenant Corey Faison, pinned down in the open seventy-five yards away and crawling for cover as two insurgents fired on him from a ridge.

Silvestri, then thirty and a private first class on his first combat patrol, thought of his daughter, Sienna, at home in Boston, and he made his decision: I'm not dying here today.

He scrambled back down the rocky trail, raised his machine gun and fired a long burst, killing both insurgents. Silvestri pulled Faison behind a rock, then stood in front of him, raking the mountainside with suppressive fire, while the lieutenant radioed for air support.

"They kept telling us, 'Hold them off, hold them off, air support is on the way,'" Silvestri says. "But air support never came. We were on our own."

Farther up the trail, ten Afghan National Army soldiers and their Marine Corps adviser also were trapped. "We're pinned down," the Marine adviser called over the radio. "We can't move from our location."

The patrol couldn't pull back to safety with the Afghans stranded up front, so someone would have to cover their withdrawal. Silvestri sucked in a breath and ran toward the gunfire.

"I didn't do it thinking I'm going to get an award for this," Silvestri says, in a heavy Boston accent. "I did it because my life was on the line, my battle buddies' lives were on the line and we weren't going to die out there; it was too early in the deployment. Fear, anger, I had every emotion running through my body at once. It was either fight your way out of here, or fight and die, but you're fighting no matter what."

The patrol had left Combat Outpost Lowell, deep in the mountains of Nurestan province, before dawn that morning. The seventeen American and twenty Afghan soldiers planned to secure a ridgeline overlooking the Warmangal Valley, a suspected transit route for weapons and fighters. But an hour into the climb, as the

85

sun broke over the mountains, the patrol stumbled into a kill zone, part of a coordinated attack against Lowell and two nearby observation posts.

As Silvestri climbed back up the mountain, he could see the Afghan soldiers one hundred meters up the trail, crouched behind rocks and taking fire from a ledge on the left side of the draw. He moved toward the rock face, where the insurgent wouldn't be able to see him, and made eye contact with the Marine adviser, who pointed out the enemy's location, about seventy feet up the mountain from Silvestri.

"The guy was popping up, letting off rounds, getting down. Popping up, letting off rounds, getting down," Silvestri says. "I stepped out and waited for him to pop back up. When he stepped out and leaned over the rock, I let a burst go and hit him the chest. He dropped his weapon and slumped over the rock."

Two hours after it had started, the firefight was over. Silvestri had shot 650 rounds as he moved up and down the mountainside. Despite the volume of fire coming from the enemy, no coalition troops were injured during the ambush.

Two months later, Silvestri earned a Purple Heart when a rocket-propelled grenade blew up next to him as he slept, peppering his legs with shrapnel.

And by the time his unit left Lowell in June 2009, Silvestri and his buddies in Alpha Troop had been attacked more than 400 times. ★

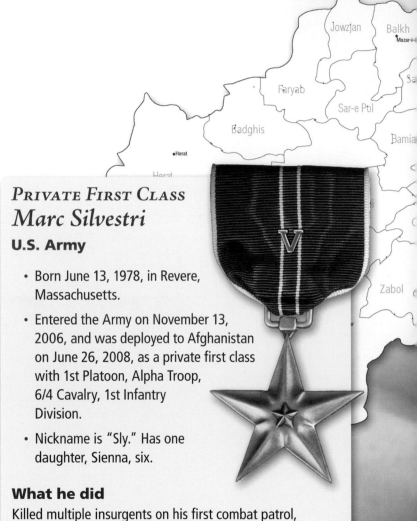

PRIVATE FIRST CLASS
Marc Silvestri
U.S. Army

- Born June 13, 1978, in Revere, Massachusetts.

- Entered the Army on November 13, 2006, and was deployed to Afghanistan on June 26, 2008, as a private first class with 1st Platoon, Alpha Troop, 6/4 Cavalry, 1st Infantry Division.

- Nickname is "Sly." Has one daughter, Sienna, six.

What he did
Killed multiple insurgents on his first combat patrol, allowing his platoon to escape an ambush.

Why he joined the Army
"It was something I wanted to do my whole life. We were at war. Now's the best time to go. Why practice and never get to play?"

(Photo by Brian Mockenhaupt)

Ronald Strickland

U.S. Army, Silver Star

By Kevin Maurer

Sergeant Ronald Strickland quickly led his team of seven paratroopers into action when a CH-47 Chinook helicopter was shot down in southern Afghanistan. (Photo courtesy of Ronald Strickland)

Sergeant First Class Ronald Strickland could just see the outline of the CH-47 Chinook as it dropped off paratroopers on the outskirts of a village in southern Afghanistan's Helmand Province.

Then he saw a streak, a flash and a fireball. The massive cargo helicopter had been shot down.

Strickland quickly pulled together his small team of seven paratroopers from the 82nd Airborne Division's 1st Battalion, 508th Parachute Infantry Regiment.

"We've got to go," he told them that day in May 2007. "Let's go right now."

Racing to the crash site, they navigated through a spider web of mud-walled compounds that eventually came to a dead end. Strickland ordered his men out of their trucks, to continue on foot. Following a mud wall, they ended up in a ditch, where they could see the helicopter on fire nearby.

Half was in a nearby compound, the rest outside the wall.

Strickland didn't know if anyone had survived but he didn't want the Taliban to get there first. (He later learned that more than fifty insurgents were swarming the area.) Strickland sent most of his men into the compound to clear it of Taliban and search for survivors. He and a medic went to the other wreckage.

Ammunition and flares cooked off from the heat. Inside the wreckage site, a thick haze of dust and smoke made it almost impossible to see. Strickland searched through the debris for survivors but found none, only seven dead bodies. The paratroopers had gotten out before the Taliban had struck.

Strickland knew he didn't have enough men to defend the site so he pulled back to a nearby intersection of two ditches, where he radioed for reinforcements.

Suddenly, two Taliban crawled out of a nearby ditch and opened fire. One had a machine gun, and Strickland could see the rounds going around a tree between them.

"I thought they were going through me," he said. Falling backward, he started to fire back with his rifle, killing the machine gunner.

The firefight lasted more than twenty-five minutes. Several times Strickland was sure he would be shot or die: "I've been in twenty-five or thirty firefights," he said. "Most times you are just reacting. You don't have time to think about stuff like that. It just lasted so long."

When reinforcements finally reached the scene, Strickland fought his way back to the trucks to link up and establish a security perimeter around the crash site.

Then he crawled back into the wreckage and recovered all the bodies. ★

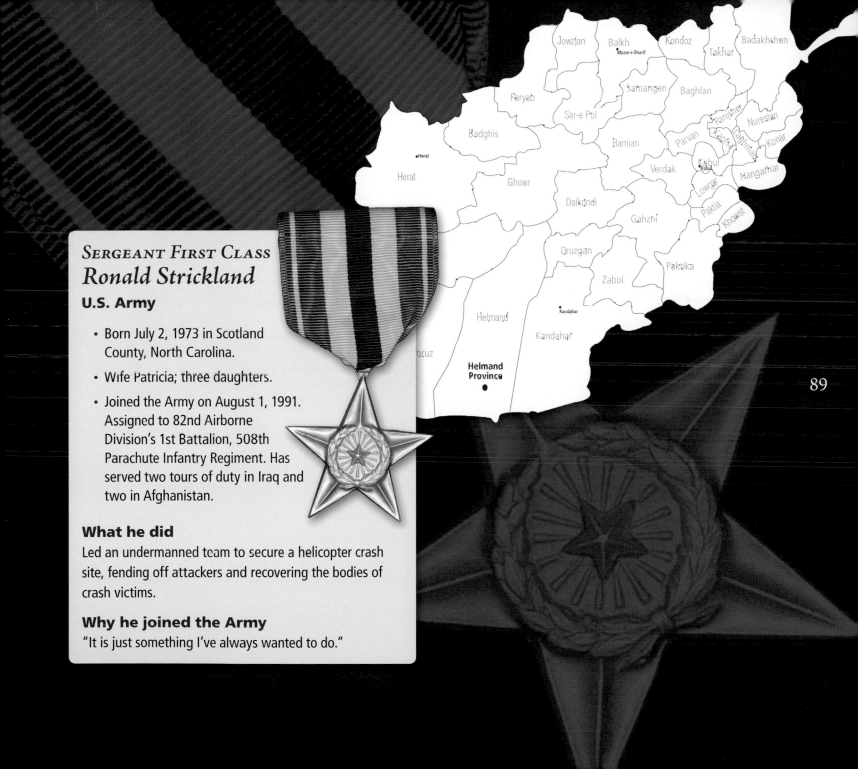

SERGEANT FIRST CLASS
Ronald Strickland
U.S. Army

- Born July 2, 1973 in Scotland County, North Carolina.

- Wife Patricia; three daughters.

- Joined the Army on August 1, 1991. Assigned to 82nd Airborne Division's 1st Battalion, 508th Parachute Infantry Regiment. Has served two tours of duty in Iraq and two in Afghanistan.

What he did
Led an undermanned team to secure a helicopter crash site, fending off attackers and recovering the bodies of crash victims.

Why he joined the Army
"It is just something I've always wanted to do."

William C. Tomlin III
U.S. Army, Silver Star

By Tim Holbert

Sergeant First Class William Tomlin III was exhausted and severely dehydrated. Up against an enemy force of 300, the forty-five soldiers of his scout platoon had been battling for nearly six hours in temperatures reaching almost 120 degrees near the village of Chakak, Afghanistan.

And now the enemy forces had closed within fifteen meters of his position.

Tomlin's platoon was part of Operation Furious Pursuit, in which 1st Battalion, 508th Infantry Regiment, 82nd Airborne Division and had been called upon to clear Taliban forces in Helmand province. Two British forward operating bases had come under siege, and it was the battalion's job to provide relief and restore security to the area.

Tomlin's unit already had been periodically engaged in combat for three days. On the morning of April 9, 2007, it was assigned a reconnaissance mission in Chakak.

Platoon leader Tomlin quickly ordered his men to set up a secure perimeter upon their arrival.

"We had started going around to the houses closest to us to clear them, and we noticed that there wasn't anybody inside," Tomlin recalled. "That's pretty common if you are about to be engaged.

"So I took a sniper team and I set them up so they could start getting their eyes away from the main element. Pretty much as soon as they got into position, the main element started receiving machine-gun and RPG (rocket-propelled grenade) fire."

The ambush, by a force six times the platoon's size, came hard and forced him to withdraw the snipers. Meanwhile, enemy fighters moved up a nearby alley directly in front of his position. Recognizing the danger, Tomlin went into action.

"I realized just how close they were, and at fifteen meters, it was anybody's game," he said, pointing out that the Americans' advantage in training and equipment was largely negated in close battle.

"I knew we had to get out of that situation. We were able to push them back down the alley with hand grenades and small-arms fire, and then we chased them down the hill into the village."

In the midst of leading the counterattack, Tomlin radioed for air support and directed reinforcements to protect his flank. Turning the tide of the battle, Tomlin's men pressed forward, driving the enemy fighters from the village until the platoon began to run low on ammunition, forcing it to break contact.

"What kept me going was the constant threat," said Tomlin, who received his Silver Star in March 2008 from President George W. Bush. "I pretty much knew that we had to stay active." Otherwise, his small force would be quickly overrun.

In the end, his platoon killed nearly fifty fighters and two Taliban leaders. No Americans died in the battle.

"I would say we were pretty lucky," he said, "and I have always said that I would rather be lucky than good." ★

SERGEANT FIRST CLASS
William C. Tomlin III
U.S. Army

• Born November 23, 1976, in New Britain, Connecticut.

• Joined the Army on May 25, 1998, and was assigned to Headquarters Company, 1st Battalion, 508th Parachute Infantry Regiment, 4th Brigade Combat Team.

• Works for the U.S. Corps of Cadets at the U.S. Military Academy at West Point.

• Has served four tours of duty overseas, two each in Iraq and Afghanistan.

What he did
Led a forty-five-soldier scout platoon that drove off a Taliban force nearly six times larger.

Why he joined the Army
"I first came on active duty in 1998. I had been simultaneously going to college and serving in the National Guard to help pay for college. When I was getting ready to graduate, I didn't really feel like I was ready to join corporate America yet, so I decided to join the active-duty Army. I told myself it would just be for three years, just to go for a little bit of fun and adventure, and it turned out that I really liked it, so I decided to stick around for a while."

William C. Tomlin

92

Jawzjan
Balkh
Kunduz
Takhar
Badakhshan
Faryab
Samangan
Baghlan
Sari Pul
Panjsher
Nuristan
Badghis
Bamyan
Parwan
Kapisa
Laghman
Kunar
Hirat
Ghor
Wardak
Kabul
Nangarhar
Daykundi
Logar
Paktya
Khost
Gahzni
Farah
Uruzgan
Zabul
Paktika
Sangin
Hilmand
Kandahar
Nimroz

Christopher T. Upp

U.S. Army, Silver Star

By S.L. Alligood

THE LOCALS HAD NOT SHOWN UP FOR WORK AT VEHICLE Patrol Base Seray on the morning of July 31, 2007, and Staff Sergeant Christopher Upp was concerned. Combined with intelligence reports of an imminent Taliban attack, the villagers' absence left him uneasy.

The day had been too quiet in the Chowkay Valley, about 12 kilometers from the Afghanistan-Pakistan border. There had not been the usual morning or afternoon attack. Now the sun was setting and the men of the 2nd Battalion of the 503rd Infantry Regiment were hunkering down for a very long night.

Then suddenly — and violently — a 107mm rocket interrupted the banter of a card game.

"Immediately after that we heard machine-gun fire going off all around us," Upp recalled.

He first thought of the 120mm mortar, about seventy-five yards away. Upp knew that if he could get his five men into the mortar pit, they stood a good chance of repelling the enemy.

"It was the main weapon that the Taliban were scared of . . . the only thing that can get them when they hide behind rocks," Upp said.

Tracer fire came from all directions as the soldiers dashed for the mortar pit. A rocket-propelled grenade exploded on higher ground, sending a wave of flesh-tearing shrapnel over their heads. As Upp and his soldiers dived into the pit, enemy machine gunners peppered the protective sandbags and rock wall with fire.

Upp remembered looking for First Lieutenant Benjamin Hall. Usually, the platoon leader was in the pit with him, barking orders on where to fire. But Hall never appeared.

"I told the men to lay low, don't show your faces and hand me rounds," Upp said.

He began firing mortars as fast as the tube could be loaded.

Several minutes into the firefight, he heard the unmistakable "thump" of a 107mm rocket being launched. Upp yelled for his men to take cover but failed to take his own advice.

The concussion knocked him to the ground. As he fell, a dollar bill-sized piece of shrapnel sliced his right arm, leaving a wide,

(Photo courtesy of Christopher Upp)

★★★
93
★★★

bloody gash. The blast also had knocked him out, but another soldier shook him awake.

Looking around, Upp realized his bleeding arm was the least of his unit's problems: The support legs and aiming device for the 120mm mortar were disabled. Now the only way to fire the weapon was to hoist the mortar tube onto his shoulders and "point and fire."

That's what he did, launching more than seventy-five rounds at the enemy.

"People in the pit were yelling, 'We're taking fire from here, here, here, here.' We were probably taking fire from four or five different locations, with twenty-five to thirty enemy fighters firing," Upp said, noting that more than twelve RPGs and more than six 107mm rockets were fired in their direction.

No others in the mortar pit with Upp were injured during the evening battle. But after the fighting ended, Hall was found nearby. He apparently had been mortally wounded during the first rocket attack.

"He wasn't more than twenty-five feet from us the whole time, behind a rock," said Upp.

He credited his unit's survival to everyone "doing their jobs and not cowering away. . . .

"What I did was probably stupid in a lot of people's eyes. I don't know why I did it; it just happened that way."

Upp doesn't like being labeled a hero. Hall is the true hero, he said.

"He was a very good officer. I don't want this to be just about me. I want it to be about everybody." ★

★★★
94
★★★

Christopher Upp stands (center in both photos) in a mortar pit with his men in the Chowkay Valley, near the Afghanistan-Pakistan border, in May 2008. (Photos courtesy of Christopher Upp)

STAFF SERGEANT
Christopher T. Upp
U.S. Army

- Born May 17, 1981, in New Smyrna Beach, Florida. His family moved to Sterling, Colorado, when he was twelve.

- Wife Melissa.

- Joined the Army in May 2000. Was deployed in May 2007 with the 101st Airborne Division, 2nd Battalion of the 187th Infantry Regiment and in August 2008 with the 2nd Battalion of the 503rd Infantry Regiment.

What he did

His right arm gashed by shrapnel, he hoisted a partly disabled mortar tube and fired dozens of 120mm rounds to repel a Taliban attack on his unit's patrol base.

Why he joined the Army

"It kind of came out of the blue. Upon graduating from high school I thought I was going to get a baseball scholarship, and it fell through at the last minute. . . . When it fell through I had no plan. I fell back on an uncle who had been in the military, and here I am. I liked it and stayed with it."

Iraq War Overview

U.S. service members were tested in several key battles — and by an untold number of attacks by homemade explosives — during six years of fighting in Iraq.

By Andrew Lubin

THE MARINES AND ARMY POURED ACROSS THE KUWAIT-Iraq border on March 19 and 20, 2003, headed for Baghdad. The faster the allies captured or killed Saddam Hussein, the thinking went, the quicker the Iraqi military would lose heart, stop fighting and surrender.

There was only sporadic and ineffectual opposition the first two days, and none was expected on March 23 as the Marines of Task Force Tarawa began to move into the city of Nasiriyah, the third-largest in Iraq.

Pentagon intelligence told the Marines that the city was friendly, but they had overlooked Fedayeen resistance forces and a large number of foreign fighters.

Task Force Tarawa's mission was to seize control of the two bridges to the north and south of the main highway running through the city so another Marine unit could pass through on its way to Baghdad.

The Battle of Nasiriyah: March 23–April 1, 2003

Iraqi artillery fire greeted the Marines as they approached the city, and having to rescue the Army's 507th Maintenance Company, which had become lost and been attacked, complicated their mission. Nasiriyah was far from friendly, the Marines quickly learned, as they were attacked by taxi loads of Iraqi soldiers and civilians in addition to the ones firing on them from the rooftops.

With Marine artillery and Marine Air Cobras shelling the city with deadly accuracy, one battalion of Marine infantrymen quickly seized the southern bridge and proceeded into the city. One company made a surprise dash up "Ambush Alley" and seized the northern bridge while under heavy fire. Two Air Force A10s added to the carnage by mistakenly firing on U.S. forces in multiple strafing runs, but the route through the city was now open.

With another Marine unit moving through the city the next day, Task Force Tarawa spent the next three days securing the city. On April 1, Special Forces, assisted by Task Force Tarawa's artillery and tanks, rescued wounded Army Private First Class Jessica Lynch from a hospital in Nasiriyah and brought back the bodies of Marines and soldiers who had been buried by the Iraqis.

With Army and Marine troops capturing Baghdad on April 9, President George Bush declared "mission accomplished" on May 1. However, American casualties from homemade bombs, or "improvised explosive devices," were increasing, and Iraq increasingly spun out of control as Shia and Sunni factions fought for control of Iraq while trying to rid their country of the "foreign invaders."

The first Battle of Fallujah: April 2004

Iraqi authorities were unable to establish law and order in the primarily Sunni city of about 425,000 located 43 miles west of Baghdad. After a Blackwater convoy was attacked on March 31, 2004, and the four Americans killed and hung from a bridge, President Bush ordered the Marines to attack the city.

In a controlled, methodical and extremely lethal fashion, Marine Air, tanks and infantry began to clear the city of insurgents. But despite the Marines being only a day or so away from sweeping through the city, Bush ordered the Marines to halt their advance and withdraw.

With the insurgents thinking they had beaten the Marines, the fighting in Anbar province and the rest of Iraq increased in lethality. IED attacks and ambushes jumped to about 300 a day against U.S. and coalition troops as casualties continued to mount. The insurgency was spinning out of control and had to be contained.

U.S. forces roll toward Nasiriyah in the opening days of the Iraq War. (Photo by Joe Muccia.) Inset, Specialist James Taylor from Munday, Texas, a cavalry scout with the 1st Infantry Division's 3rd Brigade Reconnaissance Troop, races toward a target house while conducting clearing operations in Fallujah November 15 2004, during Operation Al-Fajr. (Photo by Sergeant Kimberly Snow)

TARAWA
RAGHDAD "KEEP MOVING"

NEW YORK CITY
11309 KM

← FALLS CHURCH, VA 11513 KM
116 WEST GREENWAY TO ROCKET

WILMINGTON

11,415 KM WASHINGTON
DIRTY JERZ

← DRY

← Diamond, Oh. KB
12,129 KM

MAD TOWN, WI
CHUB 7,649 mi

At Camp Shoup in Kuwait, where U.S. forces gathered to prepare for the Iraq invasion, a signpost shows where they had been and where they were headed. (Photo by Joe Muccia)

The second Battle of Fallujah: November 2004

The Marines had this assault pre-planned, even down to the embedded media accompanying them. Attacking from multiple sides of the city, with their combat engineers turning off the electricity, Marine infantry was accompanied by tanks, air support and artillery as they began to rid the city of insurgents. The civilians already had departed, warned of the impending attack by a leaflet and microphone campaign. Block by block and house by house the young Marines kicked in doors while under fire, threw hand grenades at an enemy in the next room and often engaged in hand-to-hand fighting with insurgents hopped up on religious fervor and pharmaceuticals.

The Marines secured Fallujah, but the insurgents realized they could kill more Americans with IEDs and suicide bombers than in combat. The war deteriorated to one of sneak attacks that culminated with April 2005's huge blast in Haditha that killed fourteen Marines, all from a unit based in Brook Park, Ohio, a suburb of Cleveland.

The remainder of Anbar province and Iraq was equally dangerous for American troops, with the fighting usually consisting of an IED blast and then a firefight between the surviving Marines and soldiers and their ambushers.

But the Anbar insurgents, a combination of religious fanatics and gangsters, overreached themselves in a terror campaign, and in August 2006, a group of local sheiks led by the charismatic Sheikh Abdul Sattar Abu Risha aligned his "Anbar Awakening" movement with the Marines.

"When the Americans came, we thought they were our enemies," said Abu Risha, who was assassinated on September 13, 2007. "The awakening came when we realized the Marines were our friends."

General David Petraeus, observing how Marine-Sunni cooperation had quieted Ramadi and Anbar province in a matter of months, patterned his 2007 "surge" strategy of stationing soldiers with the Iraqi forces. The strategy was again successful, and in 2008 the newly confident government of Prime Minister Nouri al-Maliki negotiated a withdrawal treaty with President Bush that called for American combat forces to begin leaving Iraq.

President Barack Obama announced that he will pull combat soldiers out of Iraq by August 2010, leaving a residual force of between 35,000 and 50,000 troops. ★

Soldiers worship at a makeshift chapel at Camp Shoup in Kuwait. (Photo by Joe Muccia)

★★★
99
★★★

Heroes in Iraq

Elliot L. Ackerman

U.S. Marine Corps, Silver Star

By James C. Roberts

Marine Second Lieutenant Elliot Ackerman played a key role in the U.S. gaining ground in Fallujah, one of the key areas of Iraq previously controlled by insurgents. (Photo courtesy of Elliot Ackerman)

O**N THE NIGHT OF N**OVEMBER **10, 2004, AFTER A DAY** leading his men through a series of running gunfights to secure a building complex in Fallujah, Marine Second Lieutenant Elliot Ackerman got his next orders: Seize a foothold for the company deeper in the city.

For five more days, Ackerman and his platoon from the 1st Battalion, 8th Marine Regiment, would fight to the core of insurgent-controlled Fallujah, moving from one location to another while battling jihadists making a bloody last stand, hell bent to take some Marines with them.

On this night, however, the unit spotted a distant three-story building that looked to be a promising place to fight from the next day. Later finding the building partially demolished, Ackerman decided to press on. The unit camped about one hundred yards away in what they called the "candy store," a warren of four or five convenience stores under one roof.

By dawn on November 11, insurgents started milling around the street, unaware of the Marines' presence.

The insurgents soon found out.

"We were able to get a jump on significant groups trying to cross the street," Ackerman recalled. "The marksmen from the platoon were having a field day.

"Obviously it didn't take too long for the insurgents to realize where we were and at that point they started to slowly encroach and surround us."

The intensity of fire on the unit continued to escalate, he said: "It was getting pretty hairy."

Ackerman divided his platoon into three squads. One was stationed on the main floor where it exchanged fire with the attackers, while the other two remained in the basement where they rested and refueled.

At midday, the fight took a turn. A platoon sergeant collapsed after a bullet pierced his helmet, grazing his scalp. A machine gunner took a bullet in the leg that nicked his femoral artery, causing heavy bleeding.

Still under heavy fire, Ackerman called for medical help, but the first evacuation team was turned back when one of its armored track vehicles was hit by a rocket-propelled grenade. The next push, by a mobile assault platoon of heavily armed Humvees, successfully removed the wounded.

An hour later, Ackerman got new orders. Move out, his commander said. More Marines were pushing through and Ackerman's unit was to link up with them and move deeper into the city.

Since insurgents were positioned outside the front door, Ackerman ordered plastic explosives stacked against the back wall. When detonated, the blast created an opening and the platoon left the building to join their fellow forces.

A quarter-mile deeper into the city, the Marines were channeled into narrow streets. Corps tanks were blasting left and right as insurgents fired from rooftops.

The noise was deafening, but through the din came a new command: Go firm! Go firm! In other words, the Marines were to hold their positions.

"My radio operator and I just went barreling into this house," Ackerman said, and the rest of his platoon followed.

But there were insurgents on the roof. As the platoon fought to clear the house, another order to move again came as commanders wanted to reposition their tanks.

"So we had to basically move up to another street and into another house, which was a pretty hairy fight to get into there," he said.

By the end of the day, Ackerman's platoon of forty-six was down to twenty-one Marines who could fight effectively, a testament to the heavy fighting. The next day they resumed the fight to capture Fallujah, a mission accomplished a few days later.

Ackerman was awarded a Silver Star, the third highest award for valor. His Marine Corps commendation said he left safety several times to pull wounded comrades to shelter, and "rushed through a gauntlet of deadly enemy fire" to direct rescue vehicles to where his men were injured.

Ackerman also "continually attacked with his platoon directly into the heart of the enemy with extreme tenacity," the Marines said.

Ackerman was discharged from the Marines with the rank of captain and now works at the State Department in counterterrorism. ★

★ ★ ★
103
★ ★ ★

Elliot Ackerman and a fellow Marine take a break after a gunbattle near the "candy store," a convenience store that he and his platoon had occupied while insurgents roamed nearby streets. (Photo courtesy of Elliot Ackerman)

Elliot Ackerman and a fellow Marine take a break after a gunbattle near the "candy store," a convenience store that he and his platoon had occupied while insurgents roamed nearby streets. (Photo courtesy of Elliot Ackerman)

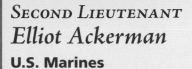

Second Lieutenant
Elliot Ackerman

U.S. Marines

- Born April 12, 1980, in Los Angeles. Now lives in Washington, D.C.

- Joined the Marine Corps on May 19, 2003. Deployed to Iraq on June 22, 2004. Had one tour of duty in Iraq (2004-2005) and one in Afghanistan (2008).

- Was assigned to 1st Platoon, Alpha Company, 1st Battalion, 8th Marine Regiment. Was a second lieutenant at the time of the incident and later was promoted to captain.

What he did
Led his platoon in a series of battles that helped his Marine Corps battalion gain a foothold in Fallujah, a key stronghold of insurgent forces in Iraq.

Why he joined the Marines
"I joined the Marine Corps to serve something larger than myself, to serve my country and my fellow Marines."

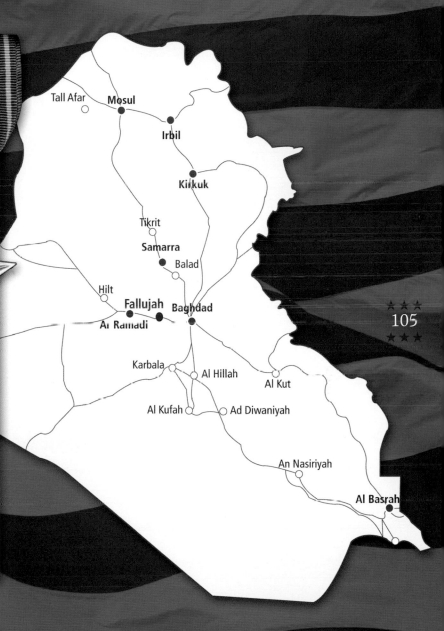

Albert R. Alvarez

U.S. Navy, Bronze Star with Valor

By Dale Eisman

THE DUST WAS ALMOST BLINDING, SWIRLING AROUND Navy Petty Officer Albert Alvarez and the Marines depending on him to neutralize two bombs they had discovered in ditches along the highway.

"We're stuck in the middle of this," Alvarez thought. "I've got to get the guys out."

The military's disposal experts disarm some bombs, destroy others by shooting at them and detonate still others. In the midst of this storm, detonation was the only option along the roadside in Iraq's Anbar province.

Alvarez figured there was a good chance he wouldn't survive.

He had left his bomb suit back at Al Asad airbase, thinking he wouldn't need it on what was supposed to be a one-day mission in the countryside. He knew his helmet and body armor would be riddled by shrapnel if the bombs exploded while he was working on them. And if he somehow survived, he probably would bleed to death since a helicopter evacuation in a raging dust storm was out of the question.

"If I get hit, I'm a goner," he said.

The first bomb actually was pretty easy. After a remote-control robot he intended to use for the job flipped over in the ditch, Alvarez eased himself down the shallow embankment and gingerly placed a timed charge of C4 explosive alongside the bomb.

He scrambled across the highway to deal with the second bomb, this one in a steeper and deeper ditch; if he crawled all the way to the bottom, Alvarez would be in over his head — literally.

Leaning on the embankment, he dangled the C4 above the bomb and tried to lower it into place. He slipped, and the charge fell.

"Oh, oh — that's a case of beer," Alvarez told himself. (The disposal team's custom is that anytime someone messes up, the offender buys a case for his squad mates.)

Petty Officer
Albert R. Alvarez
U.S. Navy

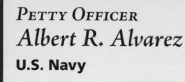

- Born June 1, 1975, in Kerrville, Texas. Lifelong Texan with a permanent home in the Dallas area.

- Wife, Julie; daughter, Isabel, ten; son, Austin, eight.

- Joined the Navy fifteen years ago and has served two tours of duty in Iraq. Stepson joined the Marines.

What he did

Safely detonated two roadside bombs in difficult terrain during a swirling sandstorm to protect a Marine mission.

Why he joined the Navy

"I originally wanted to be in the Marines because my dad was in the Marines." His father was opposed, insisting that in the Navy, "They do the same thing and have better toys."

Tal Afar
Mosul
Irbil
Kirkuk
Tikrit
Samarra
Balad
Anbar Province
Hilt
Baghdad
Rutbah
Ramadi Fallujah
Karbala
Hillah
Kut
Kufah Diwaniyah
Nasiriyah
Basra

Above left, Navy Petty Officer Albert Alvarez, had one of the most dangerous jobs in the war — explosive ordnance disposal. "It's something that nobody likes to do," he said. (Photo courtesy of Albert Alvarez)

After clearing out an improvised explosive device, Navy Petty Officer Albert Alvarez takes a break with Iraqi children in the village of Dulab. (Photo courtesy of Albert Alvarez)

But luck or something more was on Alvarez's side. The C4 fell into a perfect position atop the bomb. Alvarez clambered back up to the road, and four minutes later, both bombs were safely detonated.

The close encounter in early April 2007 helped earn Alvarez a Bronze Star medal, with a "V" device attached to denote valor in combat.

In Anbar, it turned out, Alvarez was assigned to his father's old Marine unit. "I got more time with those guys than you did," he told his dad after his last tour of duty.

Alvarez, thirty-four, got into explosive ordnance disposal after "work on the flight deck of aircraft carriers . . . just got boring."

Dealing with explosives is among the military's most dangerous work. His wife, Julie, did not care to hear much about what he did, but in 2006 she founded and still runs a Web site, eodfamilies.com, which tries to help nervous spouses cope with the stress.

An official account of Alvarez's last tour of duty in Iraq, during 2007, credits Alvarez with supervising forty-two disposal operations, clearing two hundred kilometers of supply routes and providing "the safe reduction of 2,432 pounds of enemy ordnance and explosive."

Alvarez said he doesn't think much about the danger anymore. Approaching a mission, he said, "I get kind of antsy and excited," eager to get on with the job.

"It's something that nobody likes to do." ★

James D. Ashley
U.S. Army, Silver Star

By Thomas L. Day

Specialist James D. Ashley's platoon, nicknamed Killer Troop, pulled an early morning patrol on November 12, 2008, from its outpost in downtown Mosul, arguably the most dangerous "post-surge" city in Iraq. The soldiers stopped afterward at a police station to meet with an Iraqi army unit.

As First Lieutenant Christopher Hanes went inside, the rest of his men waited outside in a courtyard in front of the station. Four armored vehicles and two Bradley tanks were parked on a nearby street. The building was well-protected from an outside attacker. But what if an attack came from inside the police station?

"I was facing away from where the incident started," Ashley said. "I was facing out. I didn't see where the gunman came from."

The gunman, dressed as an Iraqi soldier and carrying an AK-47 charged with a seventy-five-round drum, was just a few yards away from Ashley. Ashley, twenty-six at the time, reacted instinctively, his first move tackling Private Jerry Viano — at six-foot-four, a much larger man — who carried an M240 machine gun, in an effort to protect him.

As Ashley jumped on top of Viano, "that's when I was shot," Ashley recalled. The round sliced Ashley from his chin to his ear, blood hemorrhaging out of his face and covering his uniform.

Still, he continued to fight. He and other Killer Troop soldiers fired back, knocking the gunman to the ground.

★★★
109
★★★

(Photo courtesy of James Ashley)

"At that point, when I looked up, the guy . . . was still moving and reaching for his weapon," he said. Ashley had reloaded his rifle after the Iraqi soldier was shot and fired numerous times "to make sure he was no longer a threat."

Ashley and Viano then charged into the police station, joining Hanes, and checked room by room to make sure the Iraqi soldier didn't have accomplices. The other Iraqis willingly consolidated themselves into one room. Hanes feared a second attack. It didn't come.

The most seriously wounded were loaded onto the two Bradleys, destined for the nearest combat hospital. Hanes told Ashley to jump in with the next Medevac convoy. The specialist refused.

"All I knew is I was alive and breathing and these other guys were laying on the ground," Ashley recalled.

Instead of receiving first aid, Ashley helped the medics administer it. Then he jumped in a vehicle and directed his driver to the hospital. Once there, he rolled up his sleeve and begged the nurses to draw his A-negative blood for another wounded soldier.

Ashley's day, and combat tour, ended with a shot of morphine. He would be sent home the next day and later was awarded the Silver Star for his actions.

Two American soldiers were killed in the attack, and six others were injured. It could have been more.

This was Ashley's second stint in the military. His first was a short one, truncated after an injury in basic training. After a few years in law enforcement, Ashley returned to the Army in April 2006.

He said he wanted to settle "unfinished business." ★

SPECIALIST
James D. Ashley
U.S. Army

- Born May 19, 1982, in Key West, Florida, and raised in the islands of the Florida Keys.

- Unmarried, he is stationed at Fort Hood, Texas.

- Enlisted in April 2006 and deployed to Iraq on November 8, 2007.

- This was Ashley's first combat tour. He was in his twelfth month in the country; his unit was scheduled to be deployed for fifteen months, but he and much of his troop left after the incident.

- Ashley's grandfather served in the Navy during World War II.

What he did
Ashley was shot in the face as he tackled and saved a fellow soldier before helping kill the attacker. He then refused to be evacuated and helped medics tend to other wounded soldiers first.

Why he joined the Army
"I had already started the enlisted process because I wanted to be a sniper, then 9/11 happened and I just went down there and said, 'Send me as soon a possible.' "

(Photo courtesy of James Ashley)

Donald D. Brazeal

U.S. Marine Corps, Bronze Star with Valor

By Tim Holbert

THE ENEMY ATTACK BEGAN JUST AFTER SEVEN A.M., with several mortar rounds flying over the base, landing well outside its perimeter. Marines on guard duty reported some small-arms fire.

Suddenly a dump truck full of explosives headed full speed toward the base, its driver hoping to blow a hole in the perimeter. He was stopped short, the truck exploding forty meters short of its target.

The blast on April 11, 2005, shook Camp Gannon, near Iraq's border with Syria. Inside the command post, First Sergeant Donnie Brazeal, of India Company, 3rd Battalion, 2nd Marines, quickly prepared for battle.

"Needless to say, it was pandemonium from the outset," Brazeal recalled. "Multiple rockets, mortar rounds, machine-gun fire . . . you can imagine the turmoil."

The dump truck that blew up was soon followed by an ambulance filled with explosives charging toward the base, followed by a fire truck. Miraculously, the Marines managed to stop both vehicles short. Had they reached the perimeter, the damage could have been devastating.

Brazeal heard the fire truck explode. Fearing that the base had been breached, he ran toward the sound. Instead he found several of his Marines in a bunker, pinned down by about a dozen heavily armed insurgents using a nearby wall as a barrier.

Instinctively, Brazeal grabbed a rocket launcher. Another Marine followed his lead, and they climbed atop a dirt barrier. Exposing himself to enemy fire, Brazeal fired the missile toward the enemy position. The insurgents, dazed by the blast, stopped shooting, allowing the pinned-down Marines to regroup.

"When you're a first sergeant of a unit that big, you become very close with those Marines and sailors," Brazeal recalled of what was going through his mind during those moments.

"Like any good father, you never want to see anything happen to your sons, so you'll do whatever you can to protect your family."

The Marines had become a second family to Brazeal. Many of his Marines were not even born when he joined in 1983, and he felt particularly responsible for their safety. India Company saw heavy action during its tour from January to September 2005, engaging the enemy nearly 280 times.

One such action noted on Brazeal's medal citation described when a rocket-propelled grenade flew toward the position where Brazeal and his company commander, then-Captain Frank Diorio, stood.

Brazeal immediately knocked Diorio to the ground and covered him with his body, shielding him from the nearby blast.

"That man is my brother, let alone my C.O.," Brazeal explained. "He was getting ready to

Tall Afar   Mosu

Camp Gannon
Husaybah

Hilt

Ar Ran

Ar Rutbah

Below, pictured with Brazeal is his nephew, Sergeant (then Lance Corporal) Travis Gene Brazeal of Council Bluffs, Iowa. Travis was awarded the Purple Heart Medal from an injury caused by an enemy IED.

113

Irbil

Kirkuk

krit

amarra

Balad

Baghdad

bala

Al Hillah

Al Kut

Al Kufah

Ad Diwaniyah

An Nasiriyah

have his first child, and I told his wife before we left, 'At all costs he is coming home to see that child born.' "

Brazeal was awarded his Bronze Star in a surprise ceremony at the U.S. Naval Academy on January 27, 2007. In attendance were two Marines who had served under him at Camp Gannon. They had just returned from their tour. Rather than enjoy their first weekend at home, they made the trek to Annapolis, Maryland, to honor their first sergeant.

"As we say in the Marine Corps, no man is left behind, and they weren't going to leave me at this moment," Brazeal said of the ceremony. "I was very humbled and very proud." ★

FIRST SERGEANT
Donald D. Brazeal
U.S. Army

- Born May 11, 1965, in Council Bluffs, Iowa.

- Married; one daughter and two stepchildren.

- Joined the Marines on January 22, 1983. Assigned to India Company, 3rd Battalion, 2nd Marines, 2nd Marine Division. Four tours of duty overseas — two to Iraq, including the "march up" to Baghdad in 2003, and two to Djibouti. In addition to his Bronze Star with Valor, he received a Navy Commendation with Valor during his initial tour to Iraq in 2003.

- A nephew deployed to Iraq at the same time served in Anbar province. He was wounded and received the Purple Heart but recovered.

What he did
During an attack on his base, he silenced insurgents who had his men pinned down in a bunker.

Why he joined the Marines
"I come from a military family. My father was a World War II and Korean War veteran. My brothers were both United States Marines, so from an early age I strived to be a part of the military."

Jason D. Brown

U.S. Army, Silver Star

By Andrew Lubin

Jason Brown receives his Silver Star medal during a ceremony at Fort Bragg in July 2003 while his daughter Kayla enjoys the festivities.

DURING AN EARLY APRIL MORNING IN 2003, NOT LONG after the start of the invasion of Iraq, the twenty-two Green Berets of the 3rd Special Forces and their Peshmerga (Kurdish) allies were surprised by the appearance of an Iraqi armored column.

A B-52 strike on the area the night before had caused most of the Iraqi soldiers to defect, a captured officer had told them. And as the sun rose the following day, the Army unit had taken control of a critical crossroads, without a fight, on the highway linking Kurdistan's northern oilfields to the important city of Mosul.

The Green Berets had spotted the Iraqi armored column — six T-55 tanks, Soviet-style armored personnel carriers and trucks carrying soldiers — in the distance, but initially there had been no cause for alarm. The tanks had their turrets turned around, with their main guns pointing aft, in surrender mode.

Suddenly, though, the tanks swung their turrets around, opened fire and began racing toward them. Artillery fire was landing increasingly close to their position.

Staff Sergeant Jason Brown and his fellow Green Berets were in a kill zone. Their heavily modified Humvees were stuffed with ammunition and either a .50-caliber heavy machine gun or a Mark-19 rocket grenade launcher in the ring mount. That, however, was no match for the advancing force.

Brown, a weapons expert, quickly fired his Javelin, a shoulder-fired anti-tank missile, and hit one of the trucks. But the Iraqi column kept coming, and mortar shells and fire from a ZSU anti-aircraft gun burst overhead.

STAFF SERGEANT
Jason D. Brown
U.S. Army

- Born June 9, 1973, in Bartlesville, Oklahoma.

- Divorced, father of Dylan and Kayla.

- Signed his enlistment papers in April 1991. Was deployed to Iraq in February 2003.

- Was a staff sergeant at the time of the citation, now is a master sergeant.

- Was assigned to, and remains in, 3rd Special Forces.

- Since his 2003 tour in Iraq, he has done two tours in Afghanistan and another in Iraq, primarily in a training mode.

What he did
With uncanny accuracy, he fired off Javelin anti-tank missiles to stop the advance of a heavily armored Iraqi column during a key battle in the early days of the war.

Why he joined the Army
"I wanted to see the world outside of Oklahoma."

Brown was unable to reset his Javelin to quickly fire another, and the Iraqis were now less than a mile away. The Green Berets pulled back about one thousand meters to a position known as Press Hill.

"We'd decided that we wouldn't be driven off the hill," Brown recalled.

As the battle intensified, Brown and his fellow operators started filling the morning air with Javelins.

Aiming for the troop carriers, Brown was quickly three-for-three, and "as we'd hit the trucks and their troops would spill out, our .50-cals and Mark-19s were just ripping them up."

But the Iraqi artillery and airbursts continued. They were firing from miles away, and the Green Berets had no forward observers out to call in their own firepower.

Still, the Javelin onslaught and non-stop .50-caliber and Mark-19 fire finally halted the Iraqi advance.

"The Iraqis could see their trucks being taken out all around them," Brown explained, "but they couldn't find us to win it."

The Iraqi tanks pulled off the road some eight hundred yards away from Press Hill and began firing from behind embankments where the Javelins couldn't reach them.

It no longer mattered. Brown, the Army's first Javelin "ace," and his Green Berets had scored nineteen hits with twenty-two missiles. They'd torn the heart out of the Iraqi armored advance in what came to be known as the Battle of Debecka Pass. ★

Kim N. Campbell
U.S. Air Force, Distinguished Flying Cross
By Jane Erikson

THEY WERE IN A HOLDING PATTERN OVER BAGHDAD, their view of the city completely obscured by dense cloud cover. U.S. Air Force Captain Kim Campbell and her flight leader, Lieutenant Colonel Richard "Bino" Turner, had just refueled their A-10 fighters when they got the call:

Troops with the U.S. Army's 3rd Infantry Division were under attack.

"We knew that once we descended below the weather, we were in a much more vulnerable situation," Campbell recalled of that day in April 2003. "Sure enough, we started taking fire. We could see bursts coming up around us and smoke.

"It was eye-opening, to say the least."

Campbell, then twenty-seven, made a couple of passes around the target area, firing high-explosive rockets at Iraqi Republican Guard troops. Return fire stopped, and she and Turner began moving away from the combat area.

"As I was coming off target, that was when I felt and heard a very loud explosion in the back of the aircraft," Campbell recalled. "I knew immediately what happened. . . . I felt the jet shake pretty violently, and then it nosed over towards the ground, and at that point it wasn't responding to any of my control inputs."

With caution lights flashing, Campbell saw that the plane's hydraulic gauges were at zero: no brakes, no steering, no control over the aircraft.

"I looked down at the ground and saw Baghdad down below me . . . where I had just been firing at enemy forces, and thought that this would be really bad if I had to eject here."

Campbell couldn't see the hundreds of holes in her A-10's tail, but she knew the plane was built to take fire. She flipped a single switch to convert the aircraft to manual control.

"Thankfully, it worked," Campbell said, and she and Turner headed back to Al Jaber Air Base in Kuwait.

Her plane wasn't flying well, but it was flying. Controlling an injured A-10 manually with no hydraulics had been done before, but landing was another matter. Three times a pilot had attempted it. One pilot had been killed when his aircraft crashed

on landing. Another pilot survived, but his aircraft was severely damaged when it swerved on and off the runway.

But there was hope from one similar situation: the pilot had landed the A-10 safely.

Campbell rejected the option to eject once back in friendly territory: "I made the decision that I was going to try to land the airplane."

She also had time to process her reaction to what had happened.

"I tried to focus on the task at hand, but an hour is a long time and I was angry," she said. "I was angry that they got lucky and hit my aircraft. I had hoped that we had done enough to help

Captain Kim N. Campbell
U.S. Air Force

- Born June 6, 1975, in Honolulu, but she has lived in California most of her life. She considers her hometown as San Jose, where her Air Force veteran father, Chuck Reed, is mayor.

- Husband Scott Campbell is an Air Force lieutenant colonel and A-10 pilot who also has seen duty in the War on Terror. The couple have a son, Colin.

- Deployed to Iraq under Operation Iraqi Freedom March 2003. Before that, she served in Kuwait in Operation Southern Watch and in Afghanistan under Operation Enduring Freedom. In 2005 she was deployed again to Afghanistan.

What she did
Her A-10 Thunderbolt's hydraulic systems destroyed after the fighter was hit by heavy enemy fire over Baghdad, she refused to ditch the plane and defied the odds by completing a risky landing in Kuwait.

Why she joined the Air Force
"I was in the fifth grade when the space shuttle Challenger exploded, and that had a profound effect on me because I realized that they died doing something that was really important to them, and that was more important than anything else. I decided I wanted to go to the Air Force Academy, and I wanted to be a pilot in the Air Force."

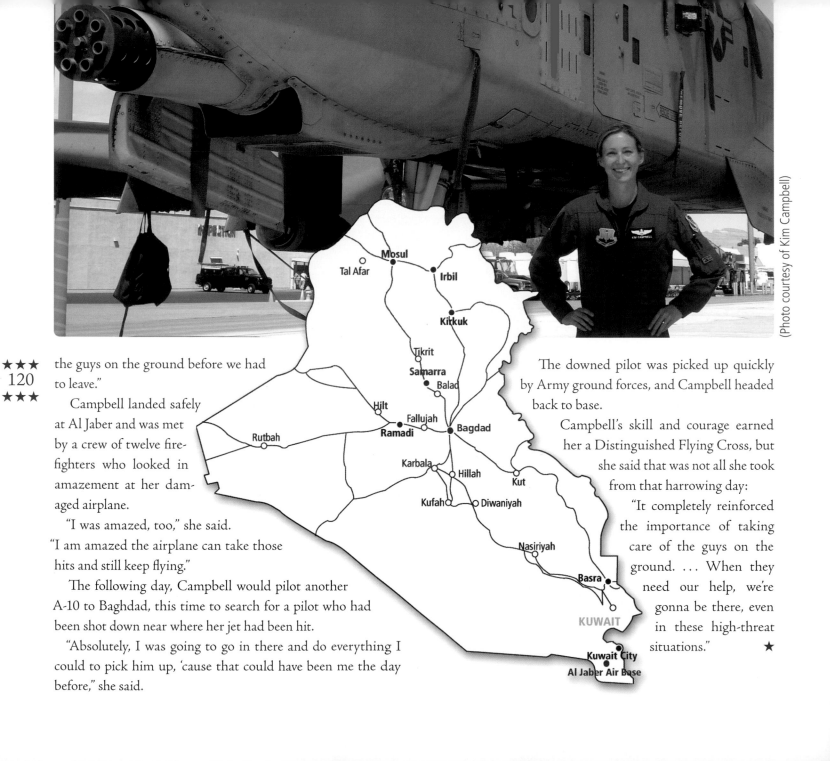

the guys on the ground before we had to leave."

Campbell landed safely at Al Jaber and was met by a crew of twelve fire-fighters who looked in amazement at her dam-aged airplane.

"I was amazed, too," she said. "I am amazed the airplane can take those hits and still keep flying."

The following day, Campbell would pilot another A-10 to Baghdad, this time to search for a pilot who had been shot down near where her jet had been hit.

"Absolutely, I was going to go in there and do everything I could to pick him up, 'cause that could have been me the day before," she said.

The downed pilot was picked up quickly by Army ground forces, and Campbell headed back to base.

Campbell's skill and courage earned her a Distinguished Flying Cross, but she said that was not all she took from that harrowing day:

"It completely reinforced the importance of taking care of the guys on the ground. ... When they need our help, we're gonna be there, even in these high-threat situations." ★

Map labels: Mosul, Tal Afar, Irbil, Kirkuk, Tikrit, Samarra, Balad, Hilt, Fallujah, Ramadi, Rutbah, Bagdad, Karbala, Hillah, Kut, Kufah, Diwaniyah, Nasiriyah, Basra, KUWAIT, Kuwait City, Al Jaber Air Base

Thomas L. Cathey

U.S. Army Reserve, Bronze Star with Valor

By Peter Slavin

THE IRAQI ARMY SOLDIERS HAD HOLED UP IN AN ABANdoned house on the morning of April 10, 2007, taking refuge from the barrage of gunfire.

Their battalion's move to seal off the Baghdad neighborhood for a building-to-building search had not gone well, as they were met by heavy resistance. Security had collapsed, and the Iraqis were down to their last magazines of ammunition.

Colonel Tom Cathey, who headed the battalion's U.S. advisory team, feared the squad would be overrun.

"There's just no way we could let that happen," said Cathey.

He knew extracting the squad would be difficult and that as soon as his rescue team left its position, "we would be surrounded 360 degrees by insurgents."

Indeed, there were several hundred of them.

The convoy of advisers — thirteen Americans and two Iraqis in four heavily armored Humvees — set out to reclaim the trapped unit. They had barely started through the streets when they surprised about ten insurgents taking a break in an alley.

Cathey's vehicle was in the lead, and his machine gunner wiped out the insurgents. At the same time, however, a grenade from a second-floor window bounced and detonated under the Humvee, blowing out the power steering and at least two tires.

The Humvee backed up so the gunner could reload. Then it pulled back into the alley's entrance, shielding the rest of the convoy and suppressing enemy fire as the other vehicles sped by.

More trouble loomed as Cathey's vehicle again took the lead. Streetwise insurgents had hurried to a second alley and set up an ambush.

"The second our bumper turned into the alleyway, the whole alley turned red with tracers," Cathey recalled. Again his gunner ended the battle.

Cathey located the trapped Iraqi squad, sorted through the confusion and loaded ten Iraqi soldiers into the Humvees. They were stacked across the back seats "like cordwood," said Cathey's driver, Master Sergeant Jack Crossman.

By now, Crossman's vehicle had lost all its tires, power steering and transmission line. Somehow, he kept it moving.

An Iraqi waved down the vehicles to report that another squad of Iraqi soldiers was pinned down in a nearby school, so Cathey's convoy responded. He positioned the Humvees to shield the front of the school, then radioed the Iraqi army to send more vehicles to evacuate the second squad.

Two Iraqi army attempts to reach the school were turned back under heavy fire.

Cathey and his men had held their ground for twenty minutes but drew more insurgents the longer they lingered.

"We were probably outnumbered at least twenty-to-one down the alleyway," Cathey said. "We were completely encircled."

Unable to hold position much longer, Cathey gave the Iraqi squad leader a choice: His men could try to escape on foot alongside the convoy or sit tight and await reinforcements. The squad leader chose to stay.

As the convoy headed back toward base, it again ran a gauntlet of enemy fire, including another grenade that exploded under Cathey's limping Humvee. After eight hours of battle, the advisory team's vehicles were battered but its personnel returned unscathed.

Cathey offered to return to the school with fresh vehicles to pick up the squad left behind. Seemingly inspired by the Americans' willingness to risk their lives, however, the Iraqi officer in charge sent his troops for the rescue.

Cathey felt rewarded. After eight months advising the Iraqi army, he said its taking responsibility in that episode was a "turning point."

Throughout the rescue, Cathey thought of the consequences if it had failed — if the marooned Iraqi soldiers had been killed, even beheaded.

"Can you imagine how the insurgents would have played that up?" he said.

And to him, the life of an Iraqi private was as important as that of a general: "They've got families, too," he said.

Crossman found Cathey remarkably calm during the fighting. Cathey said he was never scared because his team's experience and aggressive spirit made him believe they could "fight our way through almost anything."

Cathey earned a Bronze Star with the Valor attachment for combat bravery for saving the lives of ten Iraqi soldiers. His commendation read in part:

"He exhibited uncommon heroism, valor, courage, selfless service, a relentless offensive spirit to find and fix the enemy, and a common ethos among fighting men that no soldier will be left behind."

★

COLONEL
Thomas L. Cathey
U.S. Army Reserve

- Born September 15, 1962, in Waynesville, North Carolina, and is a lifelong resident of the state.

- Wife, Amy; sons Joshua, eighteen, and twins Seth and Jared, thirteen.

- Joined reserve unit in August 1980 and received second lieutenant commission in May 1982. Deployed to Iraq in June 2006 with 2nd Brigade Combat Team, 2nd Infantry Division; also served as Chief, Military Transition Team (advisory) to 4th Brigade, 1st Iraqi Army Division.

What he did
Led a convoy through a series of battles in the streets of Baghdad to rescue ten Iraqi soldiers trapped under fire in an abandoned building.

Why he joined the Army Reserve
"My dad was an Army medic before I was born. I always looked up to him as a man of character, honor and integrity. I associated these traits with those of a soldier. . . . I had looked forward to joining the military ever since I was a little boy."

Jeremiah A. Church
U.S. Army, Silver Star

By Tim Holbert

ON THE FACE OF IT, THE AUGUST 8, 2007 ASSIGNMENT TO restore the flow of water to a village near Baqubah, Iraq, seemed simple enough. Find the damage to a system sabotaged by insurgents and repair it.

But from his vantage point on a Humvee turret, Specialist Jeremiah Church began to get nervous. There was a canal on one side of the narrow road, a steep drop-off on the other. And neither left his 82nd Airborne Division reconnaissance platoon room to maneuver if necessary.

"It might sound a little crazy, but the hair on the back of my neck was standing up," he said, "and something didn't feel right in my stomach."

There was yet another sign: The children who usually flocked to convoys entering a village were nowhere in sight.

"Then I noticed a machine-gun nest off to my right that was kind of tucked off between two buildings . . ."

Fire erupted from all around. The insurgents were dug in for a well-planned ambush, and Church's Humvee was the only vehicle in position to respond with accurate fire.

Rounds smashed into the vehicles, destroying an Iraqi pickup and killing a policeman inside. Church immediately returned fire with his .50-caliber machine gun.

Insurgents had rolled a Russian DShK machine gun into the intersection ahead, closing off that escape route, but Church held firm, firing into their positions until he had to reload.

Then the enemy bullet hit him in the wrist.

"I had never been shot before," Church recalled of the firefight in which he found himself taking on more than thirty insurgents. "When I got shot I looked at my arm, and some pretty colorful language came out of my mouth. I guess the thought I had going through my head was, 'You S.O.B! I shoot you, you don't shoot me!' "

Church applied a tourniquet to his wrist and resumed firing. "That kicked my intensity level up from a ten; I probably broke the (gun) knob off the rest of the way."

Ignoring the pain and bleeding, he kept fighting, even leaving the Humvee to gather more ammunition. At one point, he began reloading with one hand, putting the injured hand inside the turret so the forward observer could apply pressure to his wound.

The damage to his wrist, however, was far worse than he knew. While the tourniquet addressed the wrist wound, an artery had been severed up to his elbow.

"In the majority of this firefight I was bleeding to death and didn't even realize it," he recalled.

Continuing to hemorrhage, Church finally passed out.

Later regaining consciousness, he got back into the fight, handing ammunition to the forward observer who had replaced Church on the machine gun.

In the end, Church's actions destroyed the enemy machine gun, enabling his platoon to join the fight. And he was credited with killing eleven insurgents.

Church said that he didn't really understand why he was receiving a Silver Star "until I realized just how much it actually meant to the people around me.

"It could have gone very wrong, real fast and real easy had I not been there, and it took a little while for that to sink in." ★

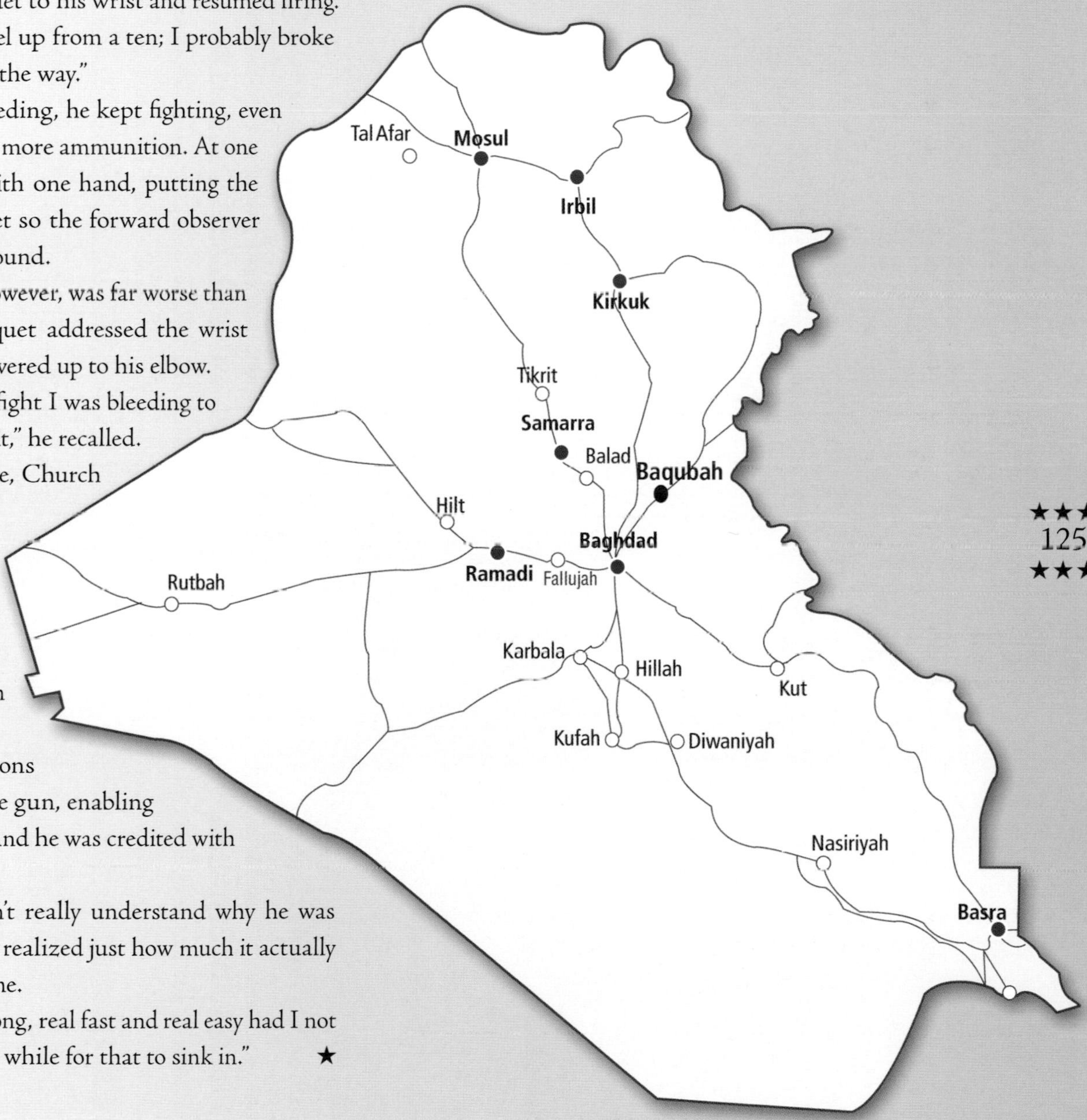

Tal Afar
Mosul
Irbil
Kirkuk
Tikrit
Samarra
Balad
Baqubah
Hilt
Baghdad
Rutbah
Ramadi
Fallujah
Karbala
Hillah
Kut
Kufah
Diwaniyah
Nasiriyah
Basra

SPECIALIST
Jeremiah Church
U.S. Army

- Born January 14, 1986, in Jamestown, New York.

- Married. Nicknames are "Jere-Bear" and "Manimal."

- Joined the Army on August 3, 2005, and deployed to Iraq exactly one year later.

What he did

Continued to fire on Iraqi insurgents even after an enemy bullet severed an artery in his wrist during an ambush. Credited with killing eleven insurgents.

Why he joined the Army

"It might sound corny, but ever since I was a little kid, as far back as I can remember, doing what I do now is the only goal that I ever had. My dream was to grow up, join the Army and go into combat. I signed up when I was seventeen, ready to go right out of high school."

Private First Class Jeremiah Church receives his Silver Star medal from Lieutenant General William Caldwell in a ceremony at Fort Bragg, North Carolina, in November 2007.

Jeremy L. Church

U.S. Army Reserve, Silver Star

By Brian Mockenhaupt

HE DIDN'T HAVE TO GO BACK OUT INTO THE KILL ZONE. He had barely made it through the ambush, and people would have understood. But Jeremy Church's friends were still out there, bleeding and dying, in a maelstrom of mortars, rocket-propelled grenades, roadside bombs and machine-gun fire.

So he went back.

"I don't think I did anything extraordinary or special," Church said of the actions that led to his Silver Star, the first awarded to a reservist in Operation Iraqi Freedom. "I know my buddies would have done the same thing if they were capable of doing it, if they weren't injured. Those men were my family, and when family members are in trouble, you help them."

The ambush had started four miles back up the road, as Private First Class Church drove the lead Humvee in a twenty-six-truck convoy escorting Kellogg Brown & Root fuel tankers to Baghdad International Airport on April 9, 2004. Enemy attacks had recently skyrocketed across Iraq, and soldiers from the Bartonville, Illinois-based 724th Transportation Company had been told to expect contact.

But no one expected this, the biggest, longest ambush of the Iraq war.

Moments after the shooting started, two rounds smashed through the windshield of Church's truck and hit First Lieutenant Matt Brown, the convoy commander, in the helmet and face. Blood poured from his shredded scalp and left eye.

It was Church's first combat experience. "When they started firing at us, that was the first time I'd ever been engaged. Far from the last, but that was the first."

He drove on tires flattened by a roadside bomb, firing his M-16 out the driver's side window. He dug out a bandage and told Brown to press it over his eye, then fielded frantic radio calls from KBR drivers whose trucks were shot up and losing speed.

"You've gotta keep going," Church, then twenty-six, encouraged them. "Just keep pushing forward."

Through mile after mile of gunfire and explosions, Church guided the convoy down the highway. Is there any daylight in this? he wondered. When are we going to get through?

Then he saw salvation: tanks and Humvees from an American cavalry unit.

Church helped Brown to a casualty collection point, then looked around. Only half the trucks had made it. His friends were still out there. So Church led cavalry troopers back into a kill zone littered with blown-up and burning trucks.

A half-mile down the road he found the assistant convoy commander's disabled Humvee,

★★★

★★★

Church is congratulated by Colonel Dan Puhl, Fort McCoy deputy commander for mobilization, upon his unit's return from Iraq in February 2005. (Photo courtesy of U.S. Army Reserve)

packed with ten men picked up along the ambush route. Most were wounded, and Church loaded them into the cavalry Humvee.

But space was tight, so Church and another soldier volunteered to stay behind. Insurgents closed in as the Humvee pulled away.

"They didn't know two of us were still there," Church says. "They thought we had all high-tailed it and left. They were talking pretty loud down in the tree line, and we just opened up on them and took care of that."

Ten minutes later, the Humvee returned. As they drove away, a rocket-propelled grenade slammed into the disabled truck, where they had been taking shelter.

The ambush had decimated the convoy. Two soldiers and seven civilian drivers died during the fight. Private First Class Matt Maupin and KBR driver Thomas Hamill had been captured.

Hamill escaped a month later from a remote farmhouse where he had been held. Maupin, Church's friend, was executed several weeks after the ambush, and his remains were finally found in 2008.

The toll could have been much higher. Church is credited with saving the lives of five soldiers and four KBR drivers, one month into the first of his two Iraq tours. ★

Church receives his Silver Star medal from Army Reserve Chief Lieutenant General James R. Helmly. (Photo courtesy of Jeremy Church)

PRIVATE FIRST CLASS
Jeremy L. Church
U.S. Army Reserve

- Born March 17, 1978, in St. Louis. Raised in Normal, Illinois now lives in Hillsborough, Missouri.

- Entered the Army in October 1999 as a military policeman. Deployed to Kuwait on February 14, 2004, and then to Iraq in March 2004.

- Deployed to Iraq for a second tour from October 2005 to the summer of 2006.

What he did

Led an ambushed convoy to safety, then returned to the battle to rescue wounded colleagues.

Why he joined the Army Reserve

"I was just looking for direction. I was a bartender and I didn't want to do that for the rest of my life. My great-grandfather was at Pearl Harbor. My cousin was in the Gulf War, so it was in the family. I just got tired of the day-to-day stuff."

George M. Collins

Arkansas National Guard,
Bronze Star with Valor

By John Lyon

(Photo courtesy of George Collins)

ON A HOT NOVEMBER NIGHT IN 2006, AS HIS PLATOON patrolled a major supply route in central Iraq to clear roadside bombs, First Lieutenant George Collins realized something was very wrong.

"We had gone through a checkpoint that was supposed to be manned by the Iraqi Army," Collins recalled. "But when we'd gone through it, it was unmanned, so we knew something was going on."

A short distance past the checkpoint, the platoon put out a robot to search a crater for improvised explosive devices, or IEDs. At the rear of the patrol, two soldiers reported seeing small-arms fire behind them, where a supply convoy had slowed to pass through the checkpoint.

Insurgents had been lying in wait to ambush the convoy. The shooting intensified, and a rocket-propelled grenade hit a supply truck. Collins, then thirty-one, acted quickly. He positioned his line of armed vehicles — including his own gun truck — between the convoy and the insurgents.

"Bullets are bouncing around off the windshield in front of us, and the gunner would flip around when he had to drop ammo," Collins said. "My driver would throw ammo up to him and then (the gunner) would spin back around.

"I've got both radios in my hand, barking out orders to my guys, trying to get . . . the convoy out of the way and seeing the window splintering in front of us."

Collins' platoon, its ammunition nearly depleted, held off the enemy until two Army tanks arrived and finished off the insurgents. The damaged convoy truck was moved out of the battle zone.

No Americans died. It is believed that eleven insurgents took part in the ambush and that all were killed, though there was never an official count.

The reality of what Collins and his men had been through didn't hit them until later.

"At that moment, adrenaline had taken over, so it didn't really bother me," he said. "But thirty-minutes later, it was pretty much a silent radio throughout the rest of the mission.

"Everybody was proud of what they had done, but at the same time you could see it in their eyes, because we had been in theater a month and never experienced anything like that."

First Lieutenant
George M. Collins
Arkansas National Guard

- Born June 23, 1975, in Martin, Tennessee, and grew up in Malvern, Arkansas.

- Wife, Lindsay; son, Emerson Collins, one; stepson Caleb Lloyd, ten.

- Inducted July 2001 and served with Alpha Company, 875th Engineer Battalion, in Iraq. Now a captain, he commands the battalion's Forward Support Company.

- Both his grandfathers served in World War II, and his father, Guy Collins of Hot Springs, Arkansas, served in Vietnam. Brother-in-law Drew Kidder of Haskell, Arkansas, has served several Iraq tours with the Marines.

What he did

Positioned his truck between insurgents and a crippled convoy, engaging the enemy so the damaged vehicles could be moved to safety.

Why he joined the National Guard

"Most of the men in my family have been in. It's just something I felt like I needed to do."

Collins received a Bronze Star with Valor, and fourteen Army Commendation Medals were awarded to his unit — 1st Platoon, Alpha Company, 875th Engineer Battalion.

One medal was awarded posthumously. Sergeant Erich Smallwood, Collins' driver on the night of the ambush, was killed in an IED explosion on May 26, 2007.

Collins wasn't there when Smallwood died, but he wears a bracelet engraved with Smallwood's name (Collins was recovering that month from an IED explosion, from which he suffered a traumatic brain injury and permanent hearing loss.).

Three years later, Collins is reluctant to accept the role of hero: "It was our job," he said.

But he is proud of what his battalion accomplished in Iraq.

"We found 1,200 IEDs. . . . That's a whole lot of IEDs that got found and detonated and didn't hurt a single person," he said. ★

★★★
132
★★★

First Lieutenant George Collins, left, takes a break with Sergeant Erich Smallwood, who was killed in an IED explosion in May 2007. (Photo courtesy George Collins.)

Robert E. Congdon
U.S. Army, Bronze Star with Valor

By Keith A. Rogers

ROCK, PAPER, SCISSORS.

That's how Army flight medics Rob Congdon and Aughe McQuown decided who would be first out the ramp of a bombed-out Stryker to face a barrage of sniper bullets. Their medical evacuation teams had been dispatched to rescue five seriously wounded soldiers twenty miles north of Baghdad along the Tigris River.

"It was just a single shooter," Congdon, a former lifeguard and paramedic from Las Vegas, Nevada, said of the thirty-five-minute ordeal on January 18, 2008.

The two staff sergeants had been dropped off a considerable distance away by Black Hawk medevac helicopters. Their pilots feared that a second roadside bomb could detonate if they tried to land near the disabled armored vehicle.

With one American soldier dead in the bomb-blast crater, the rescuers would have to take a different approach, sprinting 90 yards through tall grass to reach the wounded.

Three wounded were put on stretchers and hauled back with the help of infantrymen who had survived the explosion.

Out of stretchers, Congdon and McQuown returned to carry on their backs the last two wounded. One lay crippled on the Stryker's ramp with a broken back and shrapnel wounds to his legs.

"He couldn't walk, much less run," Congdon recalled.

Army flight medic Rob Congdon suits up for a maintenance test flight. (Photo courtesy of Rob Congdon)

That's when the sniper, hiding in a nearby building, opened fire. As bullets whizzed by their heads and feet, Congdon used his boot to push the crippled soldier back inside the Stryker. Then they ducked inside the armored vehicle and raised its ramp to close off the sniper's angle.

Congdon alertly put on the Stryker operator's helmet and radioed back to the waiting helicopters about the encounter.

The message was relayed to Apache attack helicopters that swooped in and fired 30mm cannons to suppress the sniper.

Or so they thought.

"We thought, 'All right. Cool.' So we lowered the ramp," with McQuown, slightly stockier than the six-foot-four, 220-pound Congdon, leading the way.

"It was easier for me to hang out behind him," Congdon said of his best friend, who had lost the "rock, paper, scissors" when Congdon chose rock.

"As soon as we started lowering the ramp, the guy shot at us again."

They hustled back inside. After a lull, and with an Army quick reaction force (QRF) arriving at the scene, the sniper opened up again, this time on the approaching soldiers.

"Seeing the opportunity, we tried to make it back to the aircraft," Congdon said. "Again he started shooting at us. So we went back inside, raised the ramp up and told the Apaches they need to do a little bit better job, because he's now engaging us and the QRF column."

The Apaches increased their strafing runs between the Stryker and the sniper's location.

"With that, we took off," Congdon said. McQuown went first with one patient over his back. Once McQuown made it halfway to the rescue choppers, Congdon took off with the other soldier.

STAFF SERGEANT
Robert E. Congdon
U.S. Army

- Born July 20, 1973, in Las Vegas, Nevada.

- Wife, Bonnie Kay; daughter, Samantha.

- Has been assigned to Company C, 2nd Battalion, 3rd Infantry Division, 3rd Aviation Regiment, since joining the Army. Has served two tours of duty in Iraq for Operation Iraqi Freedom.

- His brother, 1st Sergeant Michael Congdon, is an Army recruiter in Reno, Neveda.

What he did
The flight medic dodged sniper fire while rescuing wounded soldiers from an armored vehicle that had been blasted by a roadside bomb near Baghdad.

Why he joined the Army
"I joined the Army for what would be considered corny with this generation. I joined for the old-fashioned reason that it was my duty. I spent a lot of time with my grandpa as a kid, hearing his stories of his thirty-year career."

Tall Afar

Ar Rutbah

Because the soldier was so tall, Congdon said he needed help from the infantry team's platoon leader: "We kind of drug him. His feet were dangling as we ran."

About halfway to the helicopters, the gunman "figured out what we were trying to do and opened fire, but it wasn't as aimed as he had done before," Congdon said. "It was more of a 'spray and pray.' Put up enough rounds at me, and hopefully one of them hits."

They made it safely to the helicopters for a ten-minute flight to a Balad hospital, where all five wounded soldiers survived. The quick reaction force later located and killed the sniper.

In February 2008, General Richard Cody, vice chief of staff of the U.S. Army, presented the medevac team members with Bronze Star medals for valor. Congdon received his after returning from leave on March 1, 2008.

Congdon said this rescue wasn't any more heroic than others he was a part of as an infantry medic.

"It's easy to be John Wayne when you're in the infantry, because you have enough firepower to back you up," he said. "But as a flight medic, you just have your M-4 and your pistol.

"I still don't see it as anything heroic. That's my job." ★

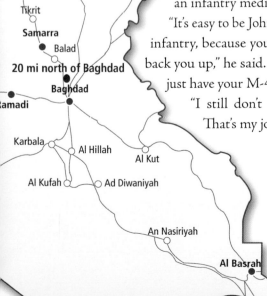

135

Rob Congdon sends a "Happy Anniversary" message from Afghanistan to his wife, Bonnie, in Las Vegas in July 2007. (Photo courtesy of Rob Congdon)

David R. Dunfee

U.S. Marine Corps, Silver Star

By Andrew Lubin

Dunfee stands near a group of weapons his Marine unit captured in Iraq.

THE FIGHT AT NASIRIYAH HAD been intense for three days. It had started Sunday morning south of the city and now, on Tuesday, Chief Warrant Officer Five David Dunfee, the battalion gunner for 1st Battalion, 2nd Marines, was north of the city.

A battalion gunner is an expert in all Marine weapons and normally would be advising his commander on the utilization of the heavy guns at their disposal. But with the 1st Battalion spread out in three different locations, there was nothing normal about this fight.

In the thick of the battle, Dunfee had directed heavy weapons fire on Iraqis fighting from the appropriately named Martyrs District; he worked with his Humvee-mounted machine gunners as they laid down a suppressing fire that, in addition to the heavy Marine artillery barrage, was instrumental in knocking out Iraqi positions.

A day of heavy fighting had secured the highway through Nasiriyah, at least enough to wave the 1st Marine Expeditionary Force through to Baghdad. But about 3:30 a.m. on Tuesday, March 25, 2003, as the heavily armored and tense Marine convoy began racing north up "Ambush Alley" through Nasiriyah, it seemingly was employing every weapon in its arsenal.

Sitting by their Humvee, Dunfee and his commander, Lieutenant Col. Rickie L. Grabowski, were startled by the volume of fire approaching them. Dunfee could hear the deep boom of .50-caliber machine guns among the higher notes of Marine M-16s and see flashes of light from tracer bullets as the convoy advanced toward them. A "friendly fire" disaster was in the offing.

As Grabowski radioed to try to halt the firing, he told Dunfee to have their company commanders mark their positions with chemical lights. The firing stopped as the convoy cleared the northernmost bridge, but as the 1st Marine Expeditionary Force vehicles drove another mile, guns opened fire again on Grabowski's dug-in Marines.

Dunfee decided it was time to act. He ran across an open field to the road, attempting to halt the friendly fire personally.

"I thought he was going to be killed," Grabowski said later. "The volume of fire directed at us was incredible."

Waving his arms wildly while ignoring the fire directed at him, Dunfee jumped into the middle of the road, forcing the lead vehicle to slam on its brakes.

"Cease fire. You're firing on Marines," Dunfee bellowed as he continued to block the passage of the heavily armed lead Humvee. As the following vehicles braked to a halt, Dunfee kept moving from side to side to keep them from passing, loudly and expressively ordering the convoy to stop firing.

★★★
136
★★★

Chief Warrant Officer Five
David Dunfee
U.S. Marines

- Born December 17, 1959, in Huntington, West Virginia.
- Married to Diana; one son, Sheamus.
- Joined the Marines on May 15, 1978, and has served two tours of duty in Iraq.
- Was assigned to Headquarters Company, 1st Battalion, 2nd Marines.

What he did

Under heavy fire, raced across a field and jumped into the road to halt an onrushing Marine convoy and head off a potential "friendly fire" disaster.

Why he joined the Marines

"My father and uncle had retired from the Navy, so I always knew I wanted to serve. But when getting ready to enlist in the Army, I met a Marine recruiter who smirked at me, and after talking with him, I knew I wanted to be a Marine."

David Dunfee, third from left, battalion gunner for 1st Battalion, 2nd Marines, made a daring — and successful — attempt to halt what could have been a disastrous "friendly fire" incident in Nasiriyah, Iraq. "I thought he was going to be killed," said Lieutenant Col. Rickie Grabowski.

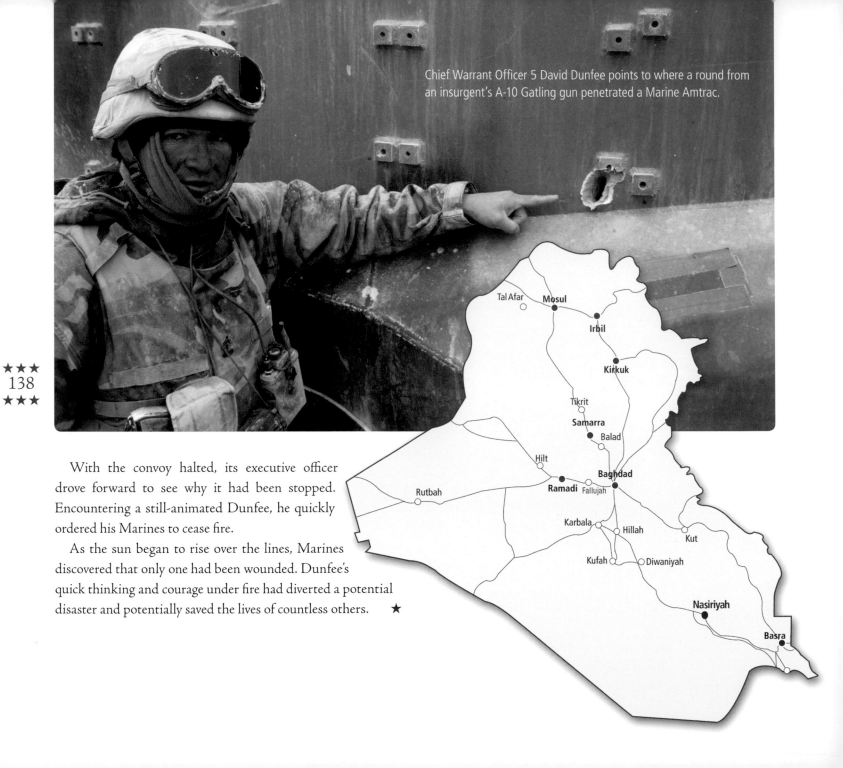

Chief Warrant Officer 5 David Dunfee points to where a round from an insurgent's A-10 Gatling gun penetrated a Marine Amtrac.

With the convoy halted, its executive officer drove forward to see why it had been stopped. Encountering a still-animated Dunfee, he quickly ordered his Marines to cease fire.

As the sun began to rise over the lines, Marines discovered that only one had been wounded. Dunfee's quick thinking and courage under fire had diverted a potential disaster and potentially saved the lives of countless others. ★

Lauralee Flannery
U.S. Army Reserve, Bronze Star with Valor
Kathryn Van Auken
U.S. Army Reserve, Bronze Star with Valor

By Kris Antonelli

Kathryn Van Auken left, and Lauralee Flannery, right.

CAPTAIN LAURALEE FLANNERY HEARD THE BOOM AND through her rearview mirror saw the mushroom cloud of black smoke and a thick hail of concrete, glass and rock come crashing down on the Kuwaiti vehicles. *Dead in the water,* she thought.

Amid the screams, smoke and chaos on February 14, 2004 on an Iraqi highway outside of Karbala, Flannery and Major Kate Van Auken had no time to contemplate their good fortune — their vehicle had not been hit.

The pair, Army Reserve officers, jumped out of their SUV and ran after the Kuwaiti civilian scientists whose vehicles had been hit by a daisy chain of roadside bombs. Bleeding, disoriented and covered with sand and dirt, the Kuwaitis were climbing out of what was left of their SUVs and wandering off the causeway into the desert.

"A couple of them were on the side of the road throwing up just from the shock," Van Auken recalled. "Some went off to pray. We wanted to keep them in front of the vehicles. It was dangerous to go off the road; it could be mined out there."

Coaxing them back to convoy vehicles was not easy — Van Auken and Flannery spoke little Arabic, and the Kuwaitis understood only a bit of English. Adding to the confusion was the language barrier between them and the Polish soldiers and Thai engineers who were trying to help. The air reeked of sulfur — a kind of rotten-egg smell that the wind carried from the craters where the explosives had detonated.

Crowds of locals were gathering at both ends of the causeway. Both women worried that there could be another attack. In those days, Karbala was a haven for insurgents, and besides the coalition forces, no one was more hated than the Kuwaitis.

As they waited for medics and support troops to arrive, the women began patching up the wounded. The Thai and Polish soldiers spread out at each end of the road and rerouted traffic. Flannery, whose last name at the time was McGunagle, directed the rest of the convoy to form a defensive circle around the disabled vehicles where the injured were being treated.

It was nothing short of a miracle that no one traveling in the twelve-vehicle convoy was killed that Valentine's Day. All the vehicles, SUVs, vans and flat-bed trucks were unarmored. The bombs, ten improvised explosive devices, had been buried in the sandy shoulder of the road at a downward angle, so when they detonated, the asphalt absorbed most of the shock.

"They were buried about five meters apart," Van Auken said. "They came right up through the engine compartment of the Kuwaitis' SUVs."

It wasn't the first time Flannery and Van Auken's convoy had encountered roadside bombs or IEDs. But this one was the most powerful they had seen.

The pair, stationed at Camp Lima, ten miles east of Karbala, had been working with a team of Kuwaiti forensic scientists excavating mass graves in the area. Their mission was to uncover as many of the 605 Kuwaiti missing prisoners of war as possible from the first Gulf War. A day before, they had received a good tip from an informant who directed them to a mass grave site outside of Karbala.

The convoy left Camp Lima early that morning and cruised slowly through Karbala to a causeway that stretched over a rocky valley to a highway on the other side. It was a beautiful morning with bright sun and clear views of the surrounding mountains.

As Flannery and Van Auken approached the causeway in the convoy's

lead vehicle, they noticed that there was no other traffic. Some trucks were stopped at a sand pit on the other side, but that seemed normal. The pair noticed that the Kuwaiti vehicles were bunching up too close together and hanging back. Van Auken got on the radio and told them to catch up but keep some distance between each vehicle. They did, and the convoy started across the causeway.

"We were about halfway across, and we just looked at each other and at the same time, realized there was still no other traffic," Van Auken said. "Then it hit. The noise was deafening. We were stunned; at first we didn't know what happened. It's almost a slow-motion sound. Everything seemed muffled. I don't know if your ears automatically shut off to protect you or what. It's like being in a tunnel."

Later, bomb technicians found the detonator — a cell phone attached to an electrical pole near the causeway.

"We didn't see it at the time," Flannery said. "We think we were being watched the whole time, and when they saw us get on the causeway, they dialed the phone and it went off."

Their near-death experience did not stop the pair from serving sixteen more months traveling around Iraq and working with the Kuwaitis to bring back their dead.   ★

Van Auken and Flannery pose in front of a helicopter.

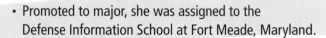

CAPTAIN
Lauralee Flannery
U.S. Army Reserve

- Born: February 21, 1962, in Placerville, California

- Enlisted in the Army on March 19, 1982 and was commissioned in June 1990.

- Deployed to Kuwait in February 2003 and to Iraq from March 2003 to June 2005. Assigned to 354th Civil Affairs Brigade, 377th Theatre Support Command.

- Promoted to major, she was assigned to the Defense Information School at Fort Meade, Maryland.

Why she joined the Army

"I came from a military family. My grandfather, my aunt, my dad were all in the military. It brings honor to my family to join, and I originally wanted to work in intelligence."

MAJOR
Kathryn "Kate" Van Auken
U.S. Army Reserve

- Born May 9, 1967, on Long Island, New York.

- Joined the Reserve Officers Training Corps at the University of New Hampshire in 1987 and was commissioned on May 20, 1989.

- Deployed to Kuwait in February 2003 and to Iraq in March 2003. Assigned to 354th Civil Affairs Brigade, 377th Theatre Support Command.

- Still active in the Army Reserve and now a lieutenant colonel, she has spent eleven years as Director of International Business Development, Department of Economic and Community Development, Commonwealth of Pennsylvania, in Harrisburg.

Why she joined the Army

"My brother got me interested. He was in the active-duty Army infantry and in the reserves as a drill sergeant. He told me about the opportunities in the military, and our family has always been pretty red, white and blue, so it was an easy decision."

What they did

Took charge of military and medical backups in the aftermath of a roadside bomb explosion that had targeted their convoy of Kuwaiti forensic scientists searching for mass graves.

Michael C. Gainey

U.S. Army Reserve, Bronze Star with Valor

By Dana Wilkie

O N THAT OCTOBER DAY IN 2007, STAFF SERGEANT Michael Gainey began a routine patrol of the Salman-Pak checkpoints southeast of Baghdad. He and his team of ten from the 211 National Police Transition Team stopped at each checkpoint to make sure supplies were in order and that inspections were being properly conducted. The team was accompanied by several dozen Iraqi police officers.

But as Gainey and his crew emerged from a wooded area near the Tigris River into an open field, bullets began raining from a three-story housing complex at the far end of the field.

Gainey had never exchanged fire with the enemy during his nine months in Iraq, but now he instantly unleashed his Humvee's M240B machine gun on the housing complex. Only when his driver, Major Edward Worthington, turned to look at him did Gainey realize something was wrong.

"You've been hit!" Worthington yelled.

"Why do you say that?" Gainey asked.

"You have blood on your neck!"

When Gainey touched the side of his neck, his hand came away covered with blood.

From left, Gainey, Major Edward Worthington, and Staff Sergeant Rodney Davenport.

His neck and hands had been hit by shrapnel after gunfire hit the metal canopy that covers the gunner's seat. Still, he didn't have time to ponder his wounds.

So heavy was the incoming fire that three soldiers about 150 meters in front of the Humvee could no longer lift their heads from the ground; if they did, they would be putting their lives in jeopardy. Bullets hailed down all around them.

"They knew if they went left or right they were taking a big chance at being shot," Gainey said. "They just lay there and kept as low as possible."

The Humvee headed straight into the thick of the attack, maneuvering to get between the downed soldiers and the incoming fire.

Relying on his training, Gainey kept moving in the gunner's seat — first up to fire a few rounds, then down, then up again. Each time he stood to aim, he was exposed from the chest up.

"It's a weird feeling that somebody is shooting at you and you can't see them," Gainey said. "You hunker down, and when you do, you say a quick prayer — 'Lord, please take care of my family (and) thank you for the life I've had' — and then you have to get yourself back together and get focused."

Finally, the Humvee got between the housing complex and the soldiers, who scrambled into the vehicle as Gainey continued to fire. The Humvee turned and headed across the field, out of range.

★★★
143
★★★

Michael. C. Gainey at the CocaCola 600 NASCAR event where he was presented with a hometwon hero award in 2008. With Gainey is his wife, Anne Marie.

Gainey was treated quickly by a medic at the battle scene, then again when his team reached its base fifteen miles away.

His Bronze Star with Valor citation for the October 22, 2007, battle said he "continually exposed himself to enemy fire" to allow his convoy to maneuver while staying clear of irrigation ditches that littered the field.

"It was an honor, and I'm very appreciative," said Gainey. "But I felt like I'd done what folks over there are doing every day." ★

STAFF SERGEANT
Michael C. Gainey
U.S. Army Reserve

- Born May 29, 1980, in Albemarle, North Carolina, now lives in Mint Hill, North Carolina.

- Wife, Anne Marie; children, Ethan and Averie.

- Joined the Army in June 1998 and deployed to Iraq in January 2007. A staff sergeant at the time of the incident — assigned to 1st Infantry Division, 211 National Police Transition Team — he is now a sergeant first class.

- Gainey today is a police officer in Mint Hill and a reservist assigned to the 98th division at Fort Jackson, South Carolina, where he trains sailors before their deployment to Iraq or Afghanistan.

What he did
Although wounded by heavy fire, he provided machine-gun cover for his Humvee to maneuver between enemy fighters and fellow soldiers pinned down in an open field.

Why he joined the Army
"I initially joined the Army for college money. The reason I stay in is for the privilege of protecting my family by defending our country from harm's way."

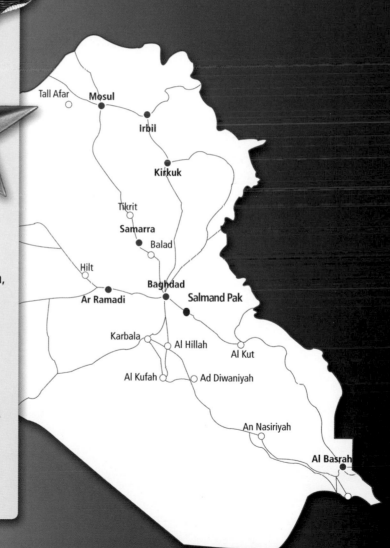

Rickie L. Grabowski

U.S. Marine Corps, Bronze Star with Valor

By Andrew Lubin

The day was not going well for Lieutenant Colonel Rickie Grabowski, commanding officer of 1st Battalion, 2nd Marines, as he stood a few hundred yards south of the railroad bridge leading into Nasiriyah, the first major city U.S. forces encountered in the invasion of Iraq.

Grabowski's Marines had lost valuable time searching for and rescuing soldiers from the Army's 507th Maintenance Company, who had bypassed their lines, taken a wrong turn and gotten lost in the city. That task had put the attack to seize Nasiriyah's bridges hours behind schedule on March 23, 2003 — the fourth day of the war.

Incredulous at what he was hearing over the radios, Brigadier General Richard Natonski, commander of Task Force Tarawa, went to the front lines to talk to his combat commander directly, as did Grabowski's commander, Colonel Ronald Bailey.

Grabowski briefed them with the best information he knew. Marine tanks and amtracs — tub-shaped assault vehicles — already had rescued some soldiers, but there was another problem. Pentagon intelligence had assured the Marines that Iraqis would be greeting them with waving flags, but the Iraqis instead were defending their city vigorously.

The attack had to proceed, but the remaining soldiers had to be found.

"Do whatever it takes," Natonski said. "Find those missing soldiers. They would do it for us, and we need to do it for them."

Grabowski quickly adjusted his plan.

With half of his big Abrams tanks refueling after rescuing some of the 507th's soldiers, Grabowski had one company and a heavily armed Humvee platoon lead the advance into the city. He and his command vehicles followed, with two other companies trailing.

But Pentagon intelligence would fail the Marines again. They encountered nine dug-in Iraqi tanks at a railroad overpass leading into the city, and suddenly the Marines were engaged, utilizing Javelin and TOW (tube-launched, optically tracked, wire-guided) missiles and blasts from low-flying Huey helicopters.

The smoke, flame and noise were incredible as the Iraqi tanks were quickly destroyed. Grabowski needed his tanks, however, as the Iraqis continued to battle.

Suddenly he heard the sounds of heavy metal moving toward him, and the ground began to rumble. Four Abrams tanks burst through the thick black smoke, seemingly out of nowhere. They raced past Grabowski's vehicle, ran up the bridge past the Humvees and amtracs and jockeyed into position in front of the Marines.

Grabbing his radio even as the tanks were moving past him, Grabowski yelled for the battalion to advance on its first objective, the Euphrates River Bridge.

Marine vehicles poured across the bridge, turning hard right and leaving the exposed road. Grabowski planned to avoid any expected Iraqi defense by advancing parallel to the main road, nicknamed "Ambush Alley," before seizing the Saddam Canal Bridge to the north.

It was a good plan, but as the tanks, amtracs and Humvees drove a few blocks, they bogged down in sewage; even the pow-

Rickie Grabowski, promoted from lieutenant colonel to colonel since the incident early in the Iraq war, now is chief of staff at Marine Corps Recruit Depot Parris Island in South Carolina.

★★★
147
★★★

Grabowski listens to a radio broadcast of President Bush giving Saddam Hussein forty-eight hours to leave Iraq in March 2003. (Photo courtesy of David Dunfee)

erful Abrams tanks broke through the hard-crusted earth and sank several feet into the stinking mess.

With the Iraqis firing down at them, the Marines defended themselves while trying to dig out their vehicles. Grabowski stood with his troops, working the radio, trying to direct his battalion while under direct fire.

Unable to free any of his tanks or 'tracs, Grabowski divided his Marines and proceeded to attack north on foot and in Humvees; his small force continued to take fire from both sides of the road and from rooftops.

Having lost much of his communications when his command vehicle bogged down in the muck under a set of power lines, Grabowski was unaware that one company commander already had made a dash three miles north to the Saddam Canal Bridge, where his Marines met heavy resistance and were mistakenly fired upon by two American Air Force A-10s.

Ducking and jabbing over the next two hours as the Iraqis continued to fire on his slowly advancing column, it took until late afternoon before Grabowski was able to reach his Marines on the Saddam Canal Bridge.

Eighteen Marines died that day. But there was little time to mourn the fallen; night was falling, and Grabowski was busy setting his defensive perimeter, planning ammunition re-supply and checking on his Marines. ★

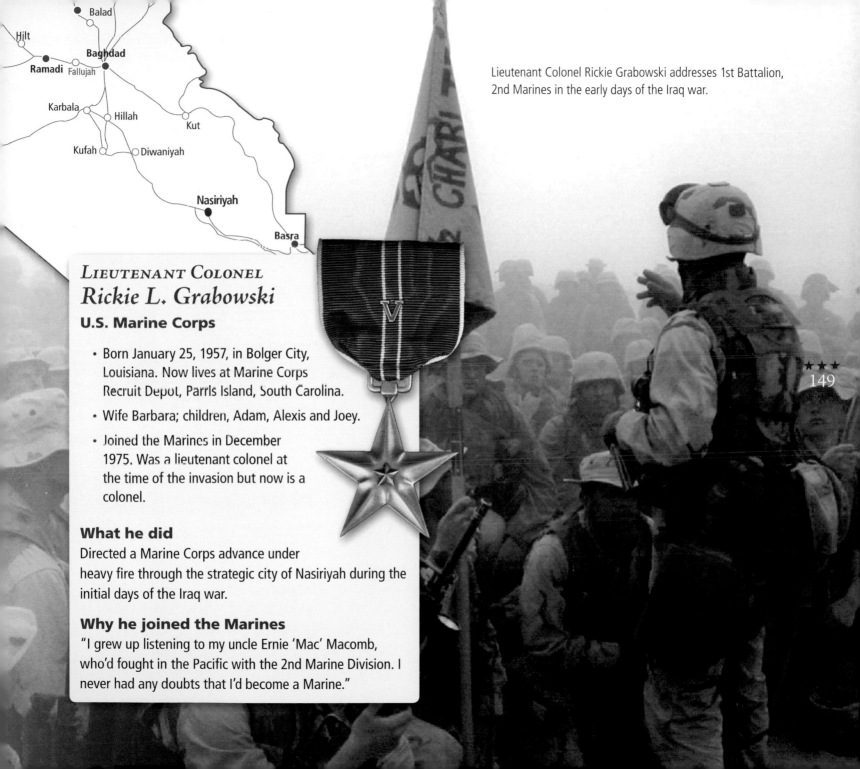

Lieutenant Colonel Rickie Grabowski addresses 1st Battalion, 2nd Marines in the early days of the Iraq war.

LIEUTENANT COLONEL
Rickie L. Grabowski
U.S. Marine Corps

- Born January 25, 1957, in Bolger City, Louisiana. Now lives at Marine Corps Recruit Depot, Parris Island, South Carolina.

- Wife Barbara; children, Adam, Alexis and Joey.

- Joined the Marines in December 1975. Was a lieutenant colonel at the time of the invasion but now is a colonel.

What he did
Directed a Marine Corps advance under heavy fire through the strategic city of Nasiriyah during the initial days of the Iraq war.

Why he joined the Marines
"I grew up listening to my uncle Ernie 'Mac' Macomb, who'd fought in the Pacific with the 2nd Marine Division. I never had any doubts that I'd become a Marine."

Robert M. Hancock

Tennessee Army National Guard, Bronze Star with Valor

By S.L. Alligood

Hancock proudly displays his Bronze Star With Valor award, which he received from Major General Gus Hargett, Tennessee Adjutant General, left, on December 1, 2007. (Photo courtesy of the Hancock family)

THE COMBINED PLATOON OF AMERICAN SPECIAL FORCES and Iraqi Army, hunting for a reported cave full of weapons south of Balad Ruz, Iraq, instead had found a cell of insurgents. Immediately, the unit was pinned down by waves of exploding mortars, small-arms fire, machine-gun fire and rocket-propelled grenades.

A short distance away, Second Lieutenant Robert Hancock heard his call sign on the radio — "Timberwolf 2!" He and his men rushed to the battle.

★★★

150

★★★

"We basically rode right into the hornet's nest," Hancock said of the men of the 278th Regimental Combat Team, a unit composed mostly of Tennessee National Guard soldiers.

That April 4, 2005, mission was the first time the combined forces of the Americans and Iraqis had worked together, Hancock said. "We knew we were going into an area where we knew we were going to receive contact."

What the Americans didn't know was that the enemy was prepared for such an incursion, and insurgents quickly immobilized two Iraqi Army gun trucks.

"Mortars were landing around us," Hancock recalled. "My gunner was squeezing the trigger just about all the time. We moved in, basically shooting everything we could see."

But the enemy, hiding in irrigation trenches, gained an initial advantage.

"RPG!" several voices screamed as one of the insurgents popped up long enough to fire an RPG in Hancock's direction. The missile sailed over his Humvee, and the Americans returned fire, taking out the insurgent.

After an F-16 jet bombed an insurgent mortar position, things quieted down — briefly.

"At that point we were doing pretty good," Hancock said. "None of us were shot. Our vehicles were hit, but no personnel were hit. We knew we had killed quite a few of them."

Second Lieutenant
Robert M. Hancock
Tennessee Army National Guard

- Born September 30, 1969, in Baltimore, now lives in Madison, Tennessee
- Wife, Tonya.
- Joined the Army in 2003. Was assigned to the 278th Regimental Combat Team, Tennessee Army National Guard. Deployed to Iraq in January 2005.
- Previously was a professional golfer.

What he did
Directed a counterattack against an insurgent ambush and helped evacuate wounded soldiers during a long firefight.

Why he joined the National Guard
"The summer of 2001, we had a friend that was working at the top of the (World Trade Center) building and never came home to see his kids. It was just one of those times I was either going to do something or not, and if I didn't, it was going to be too late. I was thirty-three at the time. I made the decision."

Thinking the majority of the enemy had been subdued, the Iraqi Army unit was given the task of sweeping the area for stragglers.

It was a mistake. As the Iraqi soldiers fanned out, a new barrage of firepower killed several of them and injured others.

Hancock, under gunfire, worked to clear the trenches where insurgents were hiding. He also retrieved downed soldiers from the battlefield.

"It was a lot of pulling guys out, calling in the medevacs, the Black Hawks, which got out all the wounded and dead," he says.

In addition, Hancock gave CPR to a fellow 278th soldier while continuing to draw fire. Unfortunately, "we lost him before the medevac even got there," he said.

Two Americans and several Iraqi servicemen died that afternoon. About 60 soldiers, both Iraqi Army and Americans, were injured in the firefight, which didn't end until the next day. There were no enemy survivors.

"It seemed like everyone, all the U.S. soldiers just banded like brothers," said Hancock, one of four 278th soldiers honored by the Army for their actions that day.

"There wasn't a man there who wasn't in the fight. I mean everyone — the gunners, the drivers, everyone — was doing what we were trained to do." ★

★ ★ ★
151
★ ★ ★

Jon M. Hilliard

U.S. Army, Silver Star

By Wesley Millett

THE FEELING OF WEIGHTLESSNESS WAS A SURPRISE. Blown out of the hatch of his Stryker vehicle and into the air, Staff Sergeant Jon Hilliard landed heavily on top of his vehicle, his head twisted in the camouflage netting. Flames licked upward from the back of the armored vehicle, and smoke poured from the troop compartment below.

"We were in column formation and moving down an alleyway between neighborhoods in Baqubah, Iraq, when we ran over a deep-buried IED," Hilliard remembered of the March 24, 2007, explosion. "The EOD (explosive ordnance detachment) guys in front had detected it, but it went off about 10 feet behind us, only seconds after we received the radio message."

The IED, or improvised explosive device, had been buried in the sewer system, a favorite location for the enemy.

Feeling an intense pain in his leg, the weapons squad leader quickly checked for blood or shrapnel. Finding none, he called down into the compartment: "Hey! Is everybody OK?"

Inside, the radio operator yelled back: "Some of the guys are hurt. We need to get them out of here!" Hilliard immediately ordered a casualty evacuation.

Caught in an alleyway, the now-immobile Stryker soon resounded with the unmistakable "ping" of enemy fire. Hilliard had to draw the attention of the insurgents.

"We were exposed like sitting ducks," he lamented.

His M203 grenade launcher was gone, and the M240B machine gun mounted in the hatch had been blown into the sniper netting. Using his knife to cut the machine gun free, he grabbed the closest box of ammunition and loaded what he had. He needed to draw fire away from the wounded being evacuated from the vehicle.

Though the M240B is designed to be mounted, Hilliard had no choice but to pick up the machine gun and fire it "Rambo-style" at enemy positions north and south of the alleyway. For two long minutes, he provided the only covering fire.

He ran out of ammo, but the platoon behind him set up a triangular defense position after realizing the Stryker had been hit.

"My only thought at the time was, 'Please don't let my men die,'" Hilliard recalled.

Hilliard had done his job: The wounded had been successfully evacuated, and his withering fire had silenced one of the enemy positions. He handed down the machine gun to one of his men and got off the vehicle, but he wasn't finished yet.

He hobbled over to the grenade launcher, now on the ground, picked it up and used it to help wipe out the last enemy machine-gun position.

When Hilliard learned that another platoon now had his unit's machine gun, he threw his assault pack on his shoulder and limped across the alleyway to retrieve it. Halfway there, a rocket-propelled grenade slammed into the ground in front of him, throwing dirt into his eyes,

Tal Afar

Rutbah

Mosul

Irbil

Kirkuk

Tikrit

Samarra
Balad   Baqubah

t

Baghdad

Ramadi   Fallujah

Karbala
Hillah
Kut

Kufah   Diwaniyah

Nasiriyah

Basra

but Hilliard charged through the doorway of the building to relative safety.

On his way back to his platoon with its weapon, Hilliard finally fell over from his injury. He refused to be carried out on a stretcher and was helped slowly to a medical evacuation vehicle, repeatedly asking about his men. Hilliard suffered serious contusions all along a leg and to an ankle. He took a month to recover.

He would later learn that seven of his men had been injured. Two lost a leg, and another had severe internal injuries.

Their staff sergeant, though, had helped save their lives. ★

Sergeant Jon Hilliard, shown here looking for weapons caches in Diyala Province, Iraq, and seven men in his platoon were wounded when a bomb blew up near them in 2007. But he kept his composure and provided covering fire to allow his men to be evacuated. No one in the platoon died from this incident.

Staff Sergeant
Jon M. Hilliard
U.S. Army, Silver Star

- Born May 5, 1981, in Chehalis, Washington. Raised in Winlock and Toledo, Washington. He is married and now lives in Winlock. His nickname is Jay.

- Joined the Army on March 15, 2000. The ambush resulting in his Silver Star occurred during his second deployment in Iraq, from June 26, 2006, to September 12, 2007. He was assigned to Company B, 3rd Brigade, 2nd Infantry Division, 5th Battalion, 20th Infantry Regiment. He was the weapons squad leader for Company B. His first Iraq deployment was from November 2003 to November 2004.

What he did
Although wounded when blown from the hatch of his Stryker vehicle, he provided covering fire to allow his men to be evacuated. Seven were injured, but no one was killed.

Why he joined the Army
"I always wanted to be a soldier, since I was a kid."

Justin D. LeHew

U.S. Marine Corps, Navy Cross

By Andrew Lubin

Tʜᴇ Iʀᴀǫɪ ʀɪꜰʟᴇ ꜰɪʀᴇ ʜᴀᴅ ɪɴᴛᴇɴsɪꜰɪᴇᴅ, ᴀɴᴅ ᴀs Gunnery Sergeant Justin LeHew ordered his amphibious assault vehicle forward, he wondered: "Who are these guys?"

The Marines had been briefed that they would find Nasiriyah peaceful, with the inhabitants "fishing off the bridges." But on March 23, 2003, the Marines found the Iraqis too busy shooting at them to be catching any fish.

Thirty minutes earlier, an American Humvee and two trucks had careened out of the city toward the advancing Marine tanks. An Army officer leaped from the Humvee, screaming about the trucks and troops he had left behind. He was the commander of the 507th Maintenance Unit, and his soldiers needed help. He had led eighteen vehicles and thirty-three soldiers into the city but had left fifteen vehicles and twenty-seven soldiers behind.

The officer eventually calmed down enough to provide some rough information about where his troops might be found. And LeHew, platoon sergeant, Amphibious Assault Battalion for Alpha Company, 1st Battalion, 2nd Marines, got the call to find them.

Driving forward in two amphibious assault vehicles, called amtracs, LeHew's platoon found one group of Army soldiers two hundred yards off the road. They had circled to surround their wounded in the middle. LeHew's corpsman, Alex Velasquez, leaped out and began treating the badly wounded as the soldiers' fire kept the Iraqis at bay.

LeHew hustled the wounded soldiers into the safety of his amtrac as his other amtrac found another group of soldiers, also with casualties, and began to load them.

The Iraqis were firing from set positions only three hundred meters away, so LeHew jumped back into his vehicle's turret and began laying down heavy fire from the .50-caliber machine gun.

This fight couldn't continue, however, as the backs of his vehicles were jammed with wounded soldiers who needed the safety of the Marine lines.

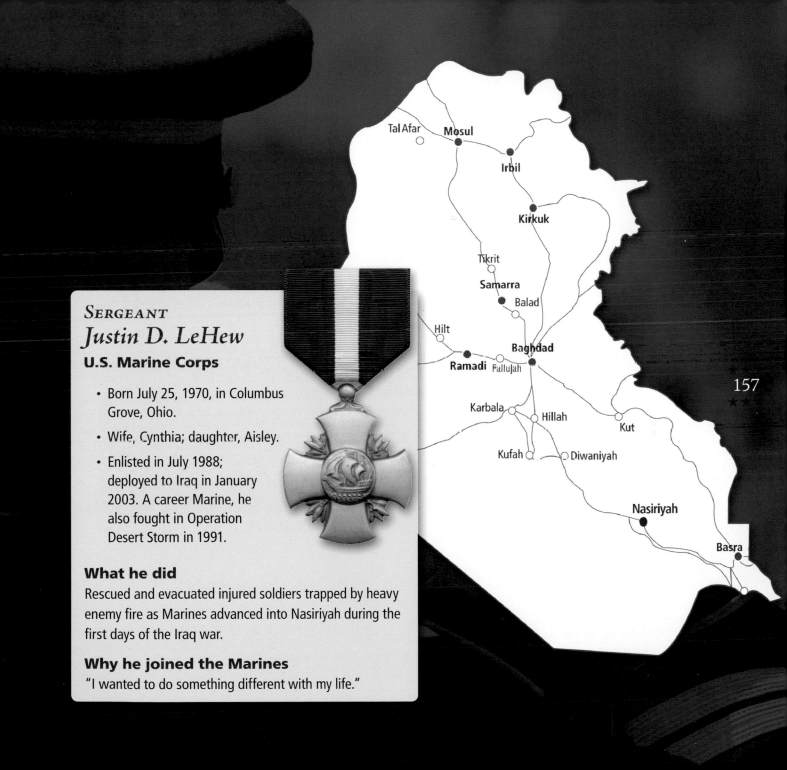

Sergeant
Justin D. LeHew
U.S. Marine Corps

- Born July 25, 1970, in Columbus Grove, Ohio.

- Wife, Cynthia; daughter, Aisley.

- Enlisted in July 1988; deployed to Iraq in January 2003. A career Marine, he also fought in Operation Desert Storm in 1991.

What he did

Rescued and evacuated injured soldiers trapped by heavy enemy fire as Marines advanced into Nasiriyah during the first days of the Iraq war.

Why he joined the Marines

"I wanted to do something different with my life."

Tal Afar
Mosul
Irbil
Kirkuk
Tikrit
Samarra
Balad
Hilt
Baghdad
Ramadi Fallujah
Karbala
Hillah
Kut
Kufah   Diwaniyah
Nasiriyah
Basra

After delivering the soldiers to safety, Alpha Company was ordered to continue the attack into the city. LeHew's unit again headed north, but the Iraqi defense stiffened as the Marines entered the city: Rocket-propelled grenades spiraled past the Marine vehicles and exploded on the road; enemies jumped out from low-slung buildings, firing their AK-47s and then dashing back to safety.

As the Marines began to dig in, the Iraqis came at them in waves. Taxicabs drove up, and young military-age men leaped out and fired.

Marine helicopter gun ships arrived, firing rockets and machine guns into groups of Iraqi soldiers. The city was ablaze in multiple spots when suddenly two Abrams tanks added to the fury, their main guns turning buildings into rubble.

LeHew spotted an amtrac crawling down the road toward the Marine position, its rear ramp bouncing off the road and throwing off sparks. Two RPGs snaked through the air toward it; both hit, and a tremendous explosion rocked the twenty-three-ton vehicle.

"I knew things were serious when a young Marine fell out the back, and he was on fire," LeHew said.

The amtrac slowed to a rolling halt, and as burning Marines stumbled and climbed out, LeHew and a medic sprinted across the street to help.

"There was diesel fuel sloshing all over," LeHew recalled, "and fire was burning next to the ammunition."

They kept digging and found a Marine alive beneath a dead body. More Marines charged across the road to help free the trapped Marine, but it still took an hour to pull him from the twisted wreckage.

This Marine lived.

Justin LeHew pauses on his tank near Nasiriyah, Iraq. Right, Gunnery Sergeant Justin LeHew and his crew take a break near Nasiriyah, Iraq, in March 2003. From left, Private First Class Edward Sasser, crew chief; Hospitalman Alex Velasquez, platoon corpsman; LeHew; and Sergeant Scott Dahn, platoon maintenance chief. (Photos courtesy of Justin LeHew)

Chad A. Malmberg

Minnesota Army National Guard, Silver Star

By Wesley Millett

THE EXPLOSION WASN'T EXACTLY A SURPRISE. RATHER, it was a fact of life along MSR Tampa, the main supply route through Iraq.

Riding in the scout truck for his column, Staff Sergeant Chad Malmberg could see that the convoy ahead had been stopped by a roadside bomb and now was under attack from small-arms fire. It was after ten p.m. on January 27, 2007, and suddenly chaos reigned all along the line, from the lead Humvee in the first convoy to the rear truck in Malmberg's own column.

As commander of his convoy escort team, Malmberg and his five up-armored Humvees had been shepherding about twenty empty semis — mostly flatbed trailers — as they returned south from delivering materials to Baghdad.

"Though it's a six-lane divided highway, the insurgents are creative in finding ways to disguise the IEDs (improvised explosive devices)," Malmberg said. "Some are camouflaged in the craters blasted out of the pavement, while others are simply hidden in the debris on the side of the road."

Soon the fighting intensified, with machine guns and rocket-propelled grenades joining the insurgents' small arms fire. That was compounded by berms on both sides of the highway that

Right, Chad Malmberg spends some time with Iraqi children on a humanitarian mission in a remote village. Left: Malmberg takes a break on a refueling stop in central Iraq. (Photos courtesy of Chad Malmberg)

prevented the semis from turning around. The road ahead had to be cleared.

As hot spots developed along his convoy, Malmberg provided support wherever he was needed most. Eventually, Apache helicopters were heard overhead.

"We welcomed their help and expected that the M280s on the helicopters would begin to rake the enemy positions by following our tracer fire," Malmberg recalled.

That hope would be fleeting.

"The Apaches weren't on the scene more than thirty seconds," he said, and for some reason they never fired on the enemy.

Malmberg could only surmise that the miscommunication was caused by heavy network traffic: "Call signs were jumping on top of each other. We simply couldn't communicate with the pilots because of the crosstalk, so I think the decision was to break off the engagement."

Whatever the reason, the convoy now was on its own. And the enemy was closing in.

"Pretty soon, we could see their silhouettes and then their faces, lit up by the muzzle flashes," Malmberg said. "They were that close."

After almost an hour of exchanging fire, the last truck in Malmberg's convoy radioed for help: Its ammunition was almost gone. Perhaps sensing that the truck was in trouble, the insurgents had closed within twenty meters and appeared to be preparing for a final assauLieutenant

Malmberg took a second gun truck with him, speeding to the rear of the line and spraying the enemy positions with heavy fire from the M240 machine guns and the .50-caliber turret guns. Then he left his Humvee to throw grenades into the ditch along the road, effectively ending the attack.

The disabled trucks in the lead convoy were cleared from the road, and Malmberg was able to move his convoy ahead. The effects of the enemy fire had been minimal, and despite the volley of rocket-propelled grenades shot at the trucks, only one did any damage.

Better yet, none of Malmberg's men had been hit, and there were no casualties. ★

STAFF SERGEANT
Chad A. Malmberg
Minnesota Army National Guard

- Born November 22, 1979, in St. Paul, Minnesota, where he still lives.
- Joined the Army on July 15, 1998, and deployed to Iraq on October 5, 2005, where he was assigned to Company A, 2nd Battalion, 135th Infantry Regiment.

What he did
Drove off enemy fighters who were closing in on a stalled supply convoy.

Why he joined the Army
"I wanted to serve my country. The military was a way for me to better my life through the Army College Fund. I also felt that the job experience gained through my training would be useful in my career."

(Photo courtesy of Chad Malmberg)

Kirkuk

Tikrit

Samarra

Balad

Hilt

Baghdad

Rutbah

Ramadi Fallujah Mahmudiyal

Karbala

Hillah

Kut

Kufah Diwaniyah

Nasiriyah

Basra

Ed Malone
U.S. Army, Bronze Star with Valor

By Tim Holbert

ED MALONE WAS READY FOR A FIGHT. THE VETERAN PLA-toon sergeant had seen enough fighting to take ground from insurgents, only to withdraw and be forced to take it again. This time, his unit had the enemy out and exposed, and it was time to make a stand.

"Let's draw these guys toward us," Malone recalled telling his platoon leader. "Let's get some support and reinforcements. And let's kick these guys' butts!"

So it went in the northern Iraqi city of Tal Afar throughout 2005. Sergeant First Class Malone had an idea what was coming during his second tour of Iraq, which began in March of that year. His first tour kicked off just after the initial push toward Baghdad in 2003, when, despite seeing some unfriendly faces in the predominantly Sunni cities of Fallujah, Hit and Ramadi, the action was fairly light.

It would be different this time around. Campaigns in Fallujah and Baghdad had driven many of al-Qaida's most hardened fighters north, where terrorist mastermind Abu Musab al-Zarqawi had a strong foothold. The citizens of Tal Afar were held hostage by ruthless al-Qaida fighters; shops closed, and the people hid in their homes.

"It just was really eerie for a town that size to have so little activity," Malone said. "And a lot of it had to do with just the amount of insurgent activity in that area."

Malone's unit – 3rd Platoon, Grim Troop, 2nd Squadron, 3rd Armored Cavalry Regiment, nicknamed "The Blue Dragoons" – was sent to Tal Afar to clamp down on the insurgency and ease the fears of the local populace.

On June 25, 2005, Malone's platoon was ordered to conduct a joint patrol with the Iraqi Army in the volatile Surai district of town. The men of 3rd Platoon had been there before and always were met with attacks. Malone had the feeling that insurgents were trying to protect something in that neighborhood.

As they entered the area, locals were conducting daily business, as children played in the street and adults walked about.

Sergeant First Class
Ed Malone

U.S. Army

- Born February 12, 1973, in Thailand but considers the Fairfield/Suisun City area of Northern California his home.

- Married with one child.

- Joined the Army on December 27, 1994, deployed to Iraq from March 2005 to January 2006, assigned to 3rd Platoon, Grim Troop, 2nd Squadron, 3rd Armored Cavalry Regiment, nicknamed "The Blue Dragoons." He also deployed there in 2003.

What he did

During a battle in a northern Iraq city, he evacuated civilians caught in the line of fire, saved a wounded comrade and led the charge into an insurgent safe house that resulted in the capture of a large weapons cache.

Why he joined the Army

"As a kid, I grew up playing G.I. Joe, running around in the woods, playing with my buddies there and pretending we were soldiers. I grew up with the idea that as a military brat I would always join the service."

But when the soldiers began knocking on doors, the people soon disappeared into their homes.

"That's usually the sign that something bad is about to happen," Malone said.

Shots rang out, and the soldiers took cover. A platoon sergeant was hit in the leg and trapped in the kill zone. Instinctively, Malone ran out and grabbed him, pulling him to safety.

Sergeant First Class Ed Malone rides in a vehicle in Iraq.

Refusing to give up ground, the soldiers held firm, beating back every assault. At one point, they noticed that much of the fire came from one nearby house. Malone knew it had to be taken. Lacking confidence, the green Iraqi soldiers refused to make the assault, leaving the Americans to do it themselves. Malone gathered his men and approached the house.

After tossing a grenade into the courtyard, the soldiers rushed inside to find a wounded insurgent and a large cache of weapons. Malone immediately provided aid to the insurgent, while the men took cover. Enemy fighters streamed toward them in an effort to recover their lost munitions.

Following a four-hour battle, Malone's unit attempted to evacuate the wounded insurgent, strapping him to a stretcher and loading him onto a Bradley Fighting Vehicle. Just then, machine-gun fire erupted from another concealed position. Malone was hit in the foot as he ran to a covered position, and he was evacuated from the fight.

Malone was awarded the Bronze Star with Valor for his actions that day. He continually placed himself in the line of fire, evacuating women and children caught in the crossfire, saving his wounded comrade and, perhaps most remarkably, providing aid to the wounded insurgent who shortly before had been trying to kill him. Asked about the latter, he put it in perspective.

"What I was thinking was, 'Well, what if this was me in the hands of the enemy?' I gave the guy treatment that I would want to receive if the roles were reversed, because I think it's just the right thing to do. And I think that represents what America is all about." ★

John A. Marra Jr.

U.S. Army Reserve, Bronze Star with Valor

By Ellen N. Woods

Staff Sergeant John Marra was inspired in battle by the memory of Corporal Rachel Hugo, a medic from his unit who was killed three weeks earlier. (Photo courtesy of John Marra)

BLASTED BY A ROADSIDE BOMB, THE LAST TRUCK IN THE convoy flew into the air and landed on its side. The gunner ran out of the dust cloud shrouding the M1117 armored security vehicle while the driver crawled out through a hole.

Two trucks ahead, Staff Sergeant John Marra Jr. grabbed his rifle and medical bag and jumped down from the turret as enemy small-arms fire peppered the wreckage. His unit, the 303rd Military Police Company, had lost its medic, killed in an ambush three weeks earlier. On October 24, 2007, with the unit nearing the end of a thirteen-month Iraq deployment, this would be Marra's first time going it alone in her place.

"I ran, apparently under a lot of gunfire," Marra said. "I could hear it at the time, but I didn't know it was skipping off the ground all around me."

When he reached the overturned truck, he found one soldier dead and another trapped. Further exposing himself to enemy fire, Marra jumped onto the passenger-side door, now the top of the truck.

Still alive inside, but in bad shape, was Sergeant First Class Christopher Blaxton, the squad leader.

"The armored doors are five hundred-plus pounds," Marra said. "Another one of our soldiers, Staff Sergeant Christopher Riley, jumped up to help me, and we held the door open while we lifted (Blaxton) vertically out the door. He weighs 200 pounds with sixty or seventy pounds of body armor and his back was broken,

so we were lifting dead weight. I did a brief check for pulse and breath, and there were no signs of life."

Marra inserted a nasopharyngeal airway tube into Blaxton's nasal passage to clear an opening. He immediately heard encouraging gurgling sounds of Blaxton attempting to breathe.

Marra's job as a military police transition team leader in the Army Reserve was to train Iraqi police. He trained hundreds of Iraqis, and two of them came to his rescue that day in Bayji, an industrial city at the northern end of the notorious Sunni Triangle.

Marra and Riley loaded their critically injured squad leader into the back of the open-bed, non-armored Iraqi police truck and raced to the district police station for further medical help.

"We were trying to outrun the insurgents," Marra said. "We were bouncing around every which way, winding in and out of alleys. I was in the back of the truck straddled on top of Blaxton, trying to cover his body while performing CPR and trying to insert an IV line."

At the same time, Marra wondered about the Iraqis in the front of the truck. He had trained them, but were they trustworthy? It wouldn't be the first time, he thought, if the drivers simply turned over their passengers to the enemy.

This time, the Marra-trained policemen delivered their cargo to safety. Blaxton survived and has since medically retired from the military. He has become a wheelchair athlete and is preparing to pursue a master's degree in business administration.

Marra dismisses his act of heroism: "Anyone in my unit would have done the same thing. We're trained to react the way we did that day. Your body takes over. The training is rigorous, and I don't think I would have been able to do what I did that day without it."

He also drew inspiration from the memory of Corporal Rachel Hugo, the medic who had been killed. She died in Bayji, in a similar attack in almost the same location.

As Marra worked to save Blaxton, he recalled a "slow-motion second" in which he "looked over at the alley where we lost her. She's the one who taught me to put in an airway. She was with all of us that day." ★

Staff Sergeant John Marra takes a break with one of his buddies, an unidentified Iraqi police sergeant. (Photo courtesy of John Marra)

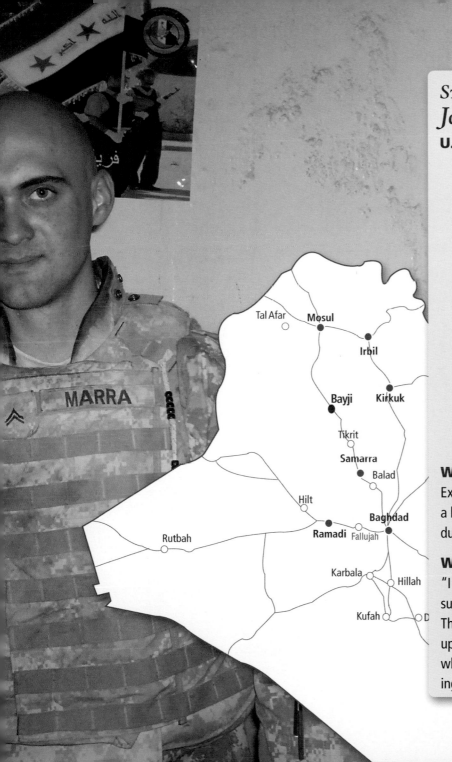

STAFF SERGEANT
John A. Marra Jr.
U.S. Army Reserve

- A lifelong Michigan resident, he was born March 19, 1978, in Trenton.

- Married to Kimberly, who began basic training in August 2009 before starting officer candidate school. They have one son, Nicholas.

- Joined the Army Reserve on September 11, 2004, and was deployed to Iraq from September 2006 to November 2007 with the 303rd Military Police Company, 785th Military Police Battalion, 300th Military Police Brigade. He has since been promoted to staff sergeant.

- A cousin served one tour of duty in Iraq and was scheduled for a tour in Afghanistan.

What he did
Exposing himself to enemy gunfire, he pulled a survivor from a bombed truck and administered life-saving medical aid during a mad dash to safety.

Why he joined the Army
"I didn't have a great job, and it was really difficult to survive at that time. I thought a lot about joining the Army. There were two wars going on, and Iraq was really flaring up. I didn't think it was fair that I would sit on the couch while other people were over there — young kids — fighting. That tied the knot for me."

★★★
169
★★★

Marco A. Martinez

U.S. Marine Corps, Navy Cross

By James C. Roberts

PINNED DOWN IN THE COURTYARD BY ENEMY FIRE COMing from inside the house, Corporal Marco Martinez and several of his Marines hid behind palm trees and returned fire. One Marine took a bullet and collapsed like a sack of bricks, alive but paralyzed.

Due to the heavy fire, the Marines couldn't risk exposing themselves to reach their fallen comrade. That's when Martinez glanced to his right and spotted a rocket-propelled grenade launcher, which had belonged to an insurgent who had been killed.

"I picked up the RPG not knowing how to shoot it," Martinez recalled. "I had only seen them in pictures and in movies. I picked it up, and in about thirty seconds I learned how to shoot it."

The grenade launcher malfunctioned twice during his quick tutorial under fire, Martinez said. "Then finally I figured out exactly what was wrong with it and shot it through the house."

The explosion temporarily stunned those inside, allowing the squad to rescue two wounded Marines. It was just one episode in a series of confrontations on April 12, 2003, in which Martinez took the lead in the town of Tarmiya, eighteen miles north of Baghdad.

Before the battle broke out, Martinez had a bad feeling about Tarmiya as he huddled with eighteen fellow squad members in the dark, confined space of their armored personnel carrier. His platoon from G Company, 2nd Battalion, 5th Marines was assigned as the reconnaissance team to scout the area.

"As soon as we got into the area you felt this weird electricity in the air, like something was not right," Martinez said.

Sure enough, as their vehicles stopped and squad members dismounted, they came under heavy fire from enemy mortars, the air thick with the suffocating smell of smoke and gunpowder.

"There were so many enemy bullets clinking on our armored (carrier) that it sounded like a Vegas slot machine that had hit the jackpot," Martinez recalled. "We took two wounded right off the bat.

"There were terrorists everywhere. No matter where you were, where you were stepping, there was someone shooting at you. It was just pure hell."

Martinez's 2nd Squad and the 1st and 3rd squads were assigned to clear Fedayeen Saddam fighters from a row of houses. The Fedayeen, paramilitary loyal to Saddam Hussein,

CORPORAL
Marco Martinez
U.S. Marine Corps

- Born September 6, 1981, in Las Cruces, New Mexico. Now lives in Los Angeles.

- Joined the Marine Corps on June 25, 2000, deployed to Iraq on February 15, 2003. Was assigned to 2nd Squad, 1st Platoon, G Company, 2nd Battalion, 5th Marines, 1st Marine Division. Was a corporal at the time of the incident, later was promoted to sergeant.

- Wrote a book, *Hard Corps: From Gangster to Marine Hero*, in which he described his teen years as a gang member before joining the military.

What he did
Took charge of his squad after its leader was wounded, leading a fierce fight against Fedayeen forces during a reconnaissance mission in a town north of Baghdad. Taught himself under fire to use a captured grenade launcher and turned the weapon onto the enemy, buying time to rescue two wounded Marines.

Why he joined the Marines
"My dad being a soldier in the Army only fueled my desire to serve. When I was in ninth grade a Marine Corps recruiter visited my high school. I was so impressed by him that I decided to join the Marine Corps when I was old enough."

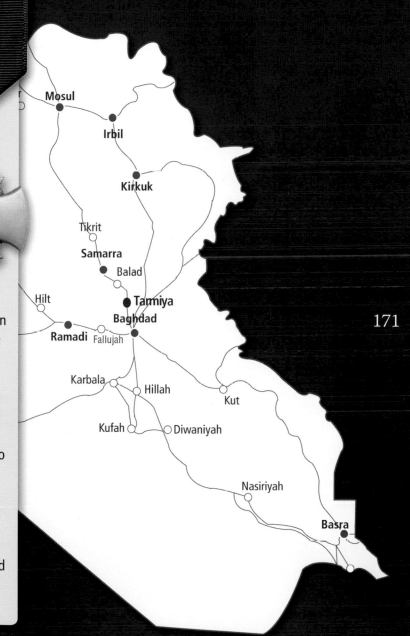

were heavily armed with AK-47s and rocket-propelled grenade launchers.

One lobbed a grenade that severely wounded Martinez's squad leader. Martinez shot the attacker as he fled. With Martinez assuming squad leader duties, the unit engaged a group of fighters hidden behind a tree line. As the Fedayeen began to retreat, Martinez and his men cut them down.

Martinez and four other Marines then entered the first house, which was filled with the enemy. Moving room to room through the three-story house, the Marines systematically cleared it out, eliminating about fifteen Fedayeen.

Following a too-brief respite in the courtyard after Martinez fired the grenade launcher, gunfire again came from the house.

"So I charged at that house by myself, firing my weapon until all my ammo was gone," he said. "By the grace of God I was not hit."

Martinez grabbed a grenade "and threw it in the window and the grenade detonated, killing some of the terrorists inside the room, and then I went inside the house and cleared out the remaining terrorists."

Martinez and his men eliminated an estimated seventy-five enemy fighters.

Martinez was awarded the Navy Cross, the second-highest honor that can be given to a Marine. He was the first Hispanic American to receive that award since the Vietnam War. ★

Michael McCarty

Arkansas Army National Guard, Silver Star
By Lewis Delavan

THE DOOR TO HIS ARMORED VEHICLE WAS DESTROYED. His radio operator lay critically wounded. Injuries incapacitated the gunner. The driver was unconscious. Shrapnel had pierced First Lieutenant Michael McCarty himself, but he knew he had to act fast.

When he spotted an enemy machine-gun crew preparing to fire on the wounded vehicle, McCarty, a farmer from Bald Knob, Arkansas, leaped from the still-moving M1114 Humvee and closed in to stop the danger.

One by one he picked off the machine-gun crew over the next few minutes, moving from cover to cover as team members supported him with fire from behind.

"I didn't have much of a choice," McCarty recalls. "Something had to be done about that machine gun."

Once the machine gun was silenced, McCarty's soldiers moved house to house in the dense Baghdad neighborhood.

"We tried to box them in, basically," he says. "There was very little room — narrow streets, people with cars on the side. We were trying to find the enemy and engage them."

McCarty was awarded the Silver Star for his actions on November 20, 2004. Many platoon members also received honors.

Left, First Lieutenant Mike McCarty was awarded the Silver Star for his actions in Iraq. His official commendation said he represents "the epitome of the American combat leader and United States Army Infantry officer." (Photo courtesy of Mike McCarty)

"They were all heroes in my book," he said. "I'm just lucky I had the soldiers I had.

"There were twenty-six heroes that day, because if any one of us hadn't done our job, then there would have been a lot more casualties than there were."

The Americans — part of Company C, Third Battalion, 39th Brigade Combat Team, attached under command of the First Cavalry, Fort Hood, Texas — faced up to one hundred combatants on that day during their mission to protect a Baghdad police station.

McCarty's vehicle was blasted when the platoon was returning to the police station. Earlier in the day, the Arkansas guardsmen lost a vehicle to enemy gunfire in the neighborhood. After depleting most of its ammunition, the platoon returned to its base to treat two casualties, repair and restock.

Upon their return, the Arkansans battled enemy fighters for an hour and a half, McCarty recalls, but "it seemed like a couple of days."

Most Baghdad houses have flat roofs, offering residents a cooling respite from summer heat. But the roofs also give insurgents a high vantage point to direct fire on U.S. soldiers.

And with most of their battalion fighting elsewhere, "There weren't many people available to help us," he said. Eventually an Apache gunship came to their aid and ended the battle.

McCarty's Silver Star commendation cited the defeat of a larger force — and much more — by the then-twenty-four-year-old officer. "His aggressive leadership, indomitable spirit, and physical courage saved the lives of his soldiers and prevented enemy forces from continuing to mass on the Zone 18 IP Station. Throughout the fight, he led from the front without regard for his own personal safety."

★★★

173

★★★

It went on to say that he represents "the epitome of the American combat leader and United States Army Infantry officer."

McCarty's twin brother, Patrick, was a sniper team leader, and the two served side by side in Iraq until the brother's unit returned home before the attack in which McCarty earned his medal.

Patrick McCarty "was honored three times for valor, so I had pretty good-sized shoes to fill," Michael says.

While grateful for the military accolades, McCarty cherishes an action by Patrick even more.

"He has a two-year boy," he says. "They named him after me. That's the biggest honor I ever had." ★

McCarty of the Arkansas Army National Guard, shown, at right, while positioned on a Baghdad rooftop in 2005, successfully led his battalion against long odds against a group of more than 100 insurgents. (Photo by National Guard Bureau)

FIRST LIEUTENANT
Michael McCarty

Arkansas National Guard

- Born January 12, 1980, and is a lifelong resident of White County, Arkansas, where he works on the family farm.

- Married Melanie Humes on September 5, 2009.

- Earned associate's degree in agriculture from Arkansas State University at Beebe and a bachelor's degree from ASU in Jonesboro. McCarty was inducted into ASU Reserve Officer Training Corps' Hall of Heroes.

What he did

Led a platoon that took on an enemy force more than three times its size, as it shielded a Baghdad police station from attack.

Why he joined the National Guard

"I joined the National Guard for the college benefits, and ROTC was a way to progress in the Guard while going to school full time."

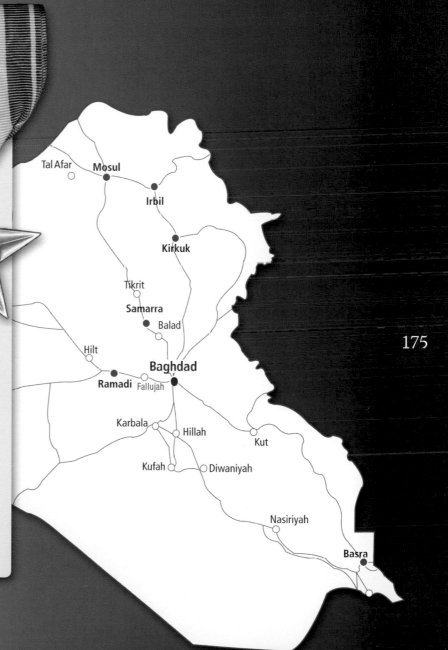

Kellie J. McCoy

U.S. Army, Bronze Star with Valor

By Kevin Maurer

O**N PAPER, THE MISSION SEEMED SIMPLE.** C**APTAIN** Kellie McCoy, on her first patrol in Iraq, was driving from the 82nd Airborne Division's headquarters outside Ramadi to a massive airbase near Fallujah to visit her troops.

"We were on our way back down Highway 10 when we started to see cars flashing their headlights," McCoy recalled. "I was just getting on the radio when the first IED went off."

The improvised explosive device set off a chain of bombs that rocked her unarmored convoy of two Humvees and two five-ton trucks. McCoy barely had time to shake off the dust when insurgents opened fire with rocket-propelled grenades and machine guns.

McCoy was commander of a headquarters company in the 307th Engineer Battalion, and her 180 paratroopers were spread all over, moving supplies around the battlefield. It was September 2003 and the insurgency was still building; roadside bombs were just appearing on the scene.

After the initial blast, thick smoke covered Highway 10, which runs east-west from the Jordanian border to Baghdad. The shock wave sent equipment flying. McCoy jumped from her Humvee and directed fire as she ran down the line of damaged trucks. She could see insurgents in the reeds firing. She watched one stand up and fire an RPG at her men.

Shouldering her rifle, she killed at least two insurgents as the paratroopers tried to break out of the kill zone.

"The situation kept getting worse and worse," she said. "That is where training kicks in. You don't have time to consider everything that is going on. You're just acting. I really do credit a lot of our training for that and making us prepared to just react in an appropriate way."

At one point, the insurgents were within twenty feet. McCoy went through several magazines, and the gunner on the last

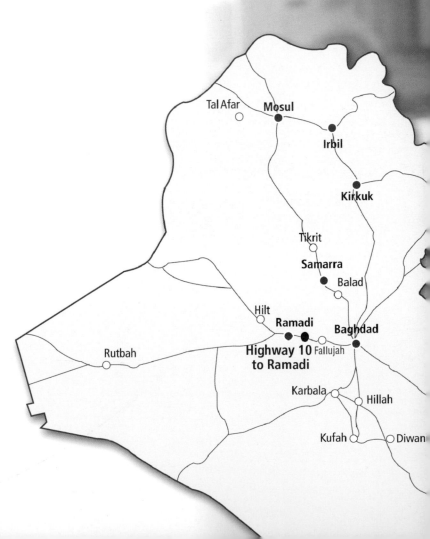

Kut

Nasiriyah

Basra

truck, armed with an M249 machine gun, fired about five hundred rounds.

"The gun was blazing hot when it was done, and he had marks on his uniform where the enemy had strafed his uniform," she said.

McCoy soon realized that three of her convoy's four vehicles were disabled. With no choice, all twelve troopers piled into a four-seat Humvee. Several had minor injuries, including concussions and ruptured eardrums. But despite the heavy fire, no one was killed.

The attack was among the first by insurgents using complex IEDs in that part of Iraq, McCoy said.

And she can't stress enough the teamwork that was involved to escape the explosions and ambush: "It wasn't just me. I was just their leader."

McCoy is now a major and on her third tour of Iraq.

"It's a six-year-old story," McCoy said of the bomb attack that led to her decoration. "This war has been going on a long time. There are lots of other soldiers and paratroopers who have performed much more heroically. I think I am just one story." ★

★★★
178
★★★

Captain
Kellie J. McCoy
U.S. Army

- Born May 1, 1975, in Akron, Ohio, has lived in Fayetteville, North Carolina, since 2001.

- Graduated from the U.S. Military Academy at West Point in June 1996, deployed to Iraq in late August/early September 2003 and has three tours of duty there.

- Was a captain and company commander, HHC, 307th Engineer Battalion, 82nd Airborne Division. Has since been promoted to major.

What she did
Led soldiers under her command to repel insurgents during a complex roadside bomb attack and ambush. All her soldiers survived.

Why she joined the Army
"I sought an appointment to West Point because I wanted a challenging and unique college experience. The notion of serving our nation and defending our freedom appealed to me then and still does. . . . There is no greater privilege or responsibility in our society than leading soldiers."

Joshua R. Mooi
U.S. Marine Corps, Navy Cross

Javier A. Alvarez
U.S. Marine Corps, Silver Star

Robert W. Homer
U.S. Marine Corps, Silver Star

By Tom Lindley

Iᴺ ᴡᴇʟʟ-ʀᴇʜᴇᴀʀsᴇᴅ ꜰᴀsʜɪᴏɴ, ᴛʜᴇ ꜰᴏᴜʀ Mᴀʀɪɴᴇs knocked on a farmhouse door, opened it and tossed in a flash grenade before rushing inside.

The morning of November 16, 2005, was another day in Operation Steel Curtain to stem the flow of mercenaries entering Iraq from Syria. The end of this particular assignment was in sight as the Marines were running out of houses to check for signs of hostiles on the outskirts of New Ubaydi, near the Iraq border.

What they couldn't know was that two dozen insurgents had picked the last farmhouse on the road for a final stand.

Or that after shielding themselves from the grenade, the insurgents would unleash a hail of explosives and gunfire on the Marines. Corporal Joshua Ware, the first Marine through the door, never had a chance: Insurgents drew a bead on him from fire ports they had cut into the walls.

There's no line on a map to etch this battle in history. What happened next boiled down to a few Marines fighting and dying to save other Marines in a battle for control of a death house in a remote spot in Anbar province.

Lance Corporal Joshua Mooi, a grenadier in the 2nd Platoon, Company F, Second Battalion, 1st Marine Corps, had just cleared a nearby house with his own fire team about fifty meters away when he heard the sudden gunfire.

Mooi, nineteen, sprinted for the house, where he found Lance Corporal Antonio Mendez outside the door, wounded.

"Where is everybody?" Mooi asked.

"I don't know," Mendez said, looking him in the eye as he continued to fire his weapon.

By the time Gunnery Sergeant Robert Homer evaded hostile fire to reach the house, Lance Corporal Lamonte McGee, who had made the dash with Mooi, had been hit in the thigh. And Lance Corporal Jeffrey Portillo had been dazed from an AK-47 round to the helmet.

"He looked like he had a baseball growing out of his forehead," Homer said.

With grenades being hurled at them from over the roof and gunfire coming at them from inside, the front of the house was no place for wounded Marines. So Homer braved more enemy fire to get Mendez, Portillo and McGee to safety.

★★★
★★★

Meanwhile, Mooi, Corporal Jeffry Rogers and Lance Corporal John Lucente went inside to rescue Lance Corporal Ben Sanbeck, who had taken shrapnel. They made the same dash across open terrain, evading enemy fire to get him to the casualty collection point.

"We're trying to find out how many people are in there, so we get as much as we can from Sanbeck and go back across," Mooi said.

Mooi's Navy Cross citation said that six times he "willingly entered an ambush site to pursue the enemy and extricate injured Marines . . . often alone in his efforts."

Mooi wasn't counting.

"I wasn't really thinking at all at this point," he said. "I was just doing what had to be done. It was nothing another Marine wouldn't have done if he was in my position."

On one trip inside the house, Mooi saw Lucente catch a couple of rounds in the stomach from one of the spider-web holes insurgents had made in the wall.

"He's in a sitting position and I'm leaned over, dragging him while Corporal Rogers is providing cover down the hallway so I can make it out," Mooi said.

They passed Second Lieutenant Donald McGlothlin, their platoon commander, who was on his way inside.

"He's asking if everybody is out," Mooi said. "I heard a couple more exchanges of fire. The last thing I heard was a loud, muffled explosion."

Mooi didn't know it at the time, but McGlothlin had taken a grenade to save them.

Outside, Rogers said they needed to go back and get the lieutenant.

Lance Corporal Joshua Mooi was described as "an amazing Marine" by comrade Sergeant Robert Homer. (Photo courtesy of Joshua Mooi)

"I said, 'What are you talking about? We just passed him up,'" Mooi said. "Sure enough, I look inside down the hallway and there's the lieutenant lying on the floor. The two of us go back in, grab the lieutenant and get him out as well."

As he walked backward, pulling the lieutenant, Mooi eyed an insurgent in the stairwell, throwing grenades over the roof into the front yard.

Mooi fired, and the man fell.

Corporal Javier Alvarez is shown on patrol in Anbar Province, Iraq.
(Photo courtesy of Javier Alvarez)

Corporal Javier Alvarez, a squad leader with two Marine units and one Iraqi fire team under his command, was on tank security when he first heard the shooting about one hundred meters away.

"We had to stay with the tanks, but once the tanks started moving that direction we followed them," Alvarez said.

Without radio communication, Alvarez couldn't tell what was happening at the farmhouse until the tank stopped.

"A staff sergeant asked me if I could have the tanks put a round into the house where the insurgents were," Alvarez said.

The tank commander wanted to know if Marines were still in the house.

That's when Alvarez saw Rogers lying face down in front of the door.

"At that point my platoon sergeant was talking to one of my teams about going in to extract Marines," Alvarez said.

There was no other way.

Alvarez took the point, firing as he ran to prevent hostiles hiding in the field from popping up and mowing them down. He was hit three times in the legs as he tried to replace a magazine.

"We continued to push toward the house, about twenty feet away at that point," he said. "I didn't know if it hit an artery, so I stopped and took cover behind the wall."

Back at the casualty collection point, Homer saw the dust fly from incoming fire from a nearby palm grove and then saw Alvarez go down, get back up and struggle to reach the house's front wall.

"It's basically kind of a lose-lose situation," Homer said. On one hand, any Marine who dared to cross the field was going to be exposed to a heavy volume of fire. On the other, there were injured Marines only thirty meters away in front of the house yelling for help.

"There's almost nothing you can do except kind of like hold your breath, run as fast as you can and hopefully you can get there," Homer said. "That's what I did."

When he arrived, Homer found himself at Alvarez's side.

Seven Marines, most of them injured, were huddled together at the wall in front of the house, still exposed to enemy fire. A Navy corpsman, Jesse Hickey, was trying to assist Rogers, and Lance Corporal Liswon Salisbury was putting tourniquets on Alvarez's legs when Salisbury, too, was shot.

★★★
181
★★★

Lance Corporal
Joshua R. Mooi
U.S. Marine Corps

- Born July 26, 1986, in Oak Lawn, Illinois, and raised in Bolingbrook, Illinois.

- Wife, Jessica.

- Nicknamed "Jinx," he joined the Marines with a delayed entry program after his junior year in high school. Served active duty from August 16, 2004, to August 15, 2008, and is still a lance corporal in the inactive ready reserves.

Why he joined the Marines

"I always wanted to join the Marines, actually, ever since I can remember. I had an uncle way back who was in the Army in Vietnam, and he used to tell war stories about how he got his foot blown off by a land mine and they had to find it and reattach it."

Corporal
Javier A. Alvarez
U.S. Marine Corps

- Born November 30, 1980, in Colombia, South America.

- Wife, Rebekah. They are expecting a child.

- Earned valor medal as 2nd Squad Leader in the 2nd Platoon, Fox Company, 2nd Battalion, 1st Marine Regiment. Served three tours in Iraq. Two brothers-in-law also are Marines — Sergeant Anthony Dilling, still on active duty, and Staff Sergeant Peter Madigral, in Marine reserves. Both also did three tours.

Why he joined the Marines

"I joined before 9/11 occurred . . . really didn't have much going on in my life at that point, and I felt the Marine Corps was the best branch of the military . . . because of their attitude, their integrity, their judgment."

Sergeant
Robert William Homer
U.S. Marine Corps

- Born October 28, 1977, in Mankato, Minnesota

- Wife, Malin; daughter, Nora, five; son, Morgan, two.

- Joined the Marines on September 16, 1992, and has served two tours of duty in Iraq. Received Silver Star while serving as sergeant, Second Platoon, Fox Company, 2nd Battalion, 1st Marines.

Why he joined the Marines

"I did not want to go to college at the time."

"It probably ricocheted off him, so I picked up my weapon and started shooting into the windows where the round came from," Alvarez said.

"As I ran out of rounds, I put my weapon down. And as I looked back up, I see Lance Corporal Salisbury's face, you know, with a pretty intense look. I look down to see what he's looking at . . . and there was a grenade."

It was rocking back and forth on the ground by the time Salisbury started yelling, "Grenade! Grenade! Grenade!"

From his sitting position, Alvarez reached for it.

"The first thing I thought was I had two or three seconds before the grenade goes off," Alvarez said. "I kind of knew where everybody was, so I knew the only place I could get rid of it. It took a little longer to turn all the way around."

The grenade exploded, blowing off his right hand.

Alvarez blacked out for a second from blast's G-force.

"As my vision came back in, I saw my hand burning, and I looked at it and it was completely missing," he said. "My sleeves were black and red from the blood. I think it was singed off, so it wasn't bleeding profusely."

Homer, sitting to Alvarez's left when the grenade exploded, was sprayed with fifteen or twenty pieces of shrapnel.

Homer took one look at Alvarez and took his belt off because "we're running low on tourniquets and there's a lot of bleeding going on."

Alvarez was too big for Homer to carry and there were too many bullets flying to risk removing Alvarez's flak jacket, so he got him to his feet.

"Hey, you gotta help me out here," Homer told Alvarez. "You gotta stand up. I know you have some bullet holes in your leg and you just lost your hand."

At least no more grenades came their way. Mooi had made sure of that by taking down the insurgent at the stairwell.

Mooi went back to the house one more time to link up with Rogers, only to find him dead.

"I'm a little heated and upset at this point, because

Sergeant Robert Homer, left, surveys the landscape with platoon commander Second Lieutenant Donald McGlothlin, who later took a grenade to save his men. (Photo courtesy of Robert Homer)

Gunnery Sergeant Robert Homer
(Photo courtesy of U.S. Marine Corps)

★★★
183
★★★

Joshua Mooi, Robert Homer, Javier Alvarez and Hospitalman Jesse Hickey prepare to receive their medals on January 8, 2009, at Camp Pendleton near San Diego. Mooi was awarded the Navy Cross; the others received Silver Stars. (Photo courtesy of U.S. Marine Corps)

I'm the only person left from my squad," said Mooi, who then fired a rocket-propelled grenade through the door and stormed in with Lance Corporal Justin Mayfield.

They cleared three rooms and the stairwell before going out back, where another insurgent had Mooi in his sights. Mooi traded fire until his M-16 jammed.

Nicknamed "Jinx" because his good luck didn't always rub off on everyone else, Mooi figured his own luck had run out, too.

But the bullet struck Mooi's rifle, giving Mayfield time to raise his weapon and kill the insurgent.

Altogether, "Jinx" was shot three times in the weapon that day.

"He didn't go down," Homer said. "He's the man, I guess, an amazing Marine."

Afterward, with rescue helicopters whirling around him, Mooi ended up on the roof of the casualty collection point. Downstairs, a staff sergeant was taking a head count. He found the First Squad in one room, Second Squad in another.

"Where's Third Squad?" he said.

"I'm up here," Mooi replied.

He gave Mooi an incredulous look, as if to ask what happened to everybody else.

"I don't know," Mooi said.

Five Marines died that day. Eleven others were injured.

The record also shows that Mooi's actions helped save ten Marines and brought an end to a little-known firefight as part of Operation Steel Curtain.

It lasted only an hour, but the heroics produced one Navy Cross, four Silver Stars and three Bronze Stars with Valor.   ★

Nicole P. O'Hara

U.S. Air Force, Bronze Star with Valor

Christopher D. Willson

U.S. Air Force, Bronze Star with Valor

By Kris Antonelli

PEERING THROUGH A GAP IN THE GUN TURRET, AIRMAN First Class Nicole O'Hara adjusted her night-vision goggles. She spotted the murky-green outlines of a gunman firing from behind a sparse tree line on the left side of the highway.

Heart and head pounding, the twenty-one-year-old O'Hara returned fire, popping off dozens of rounds from her .50- caliber machine gun. The sky, pitch black just seconds earlier, was lit up by arcs of tracer fire.

"Keep your head down!" Staff Sergeant Christopher Willson screamed up at her while driving the Humvee and working the radio. "Stay low!"

O'Hara crouched as low as she could. Tracer rounds were coming from both sides of road. Willson, then only twenty-two, slapped O'Hara's right leg.

"We have contact on the right," he yelled, his voice barely audible amid the of crash of gunfire,

the roaring engines and sharp radio commands to keep moving out of the kill zone.

O'Hara turned her gun to the right, snapping off more rounds in the direction of the tracer fire. A machine gunner in a Humvee farther ahead in the convoy already had unloaded all his rounds and was firing his M-4 carbine. Bullets bounced off the vehicles and O'Hara's armored turret as the convoy kept speeding down the highway.

But neither O'Hara nor Willson felt the speed. Instead, it felt as if everything and everyone were moving in slow motion.

Willson and O'Hara were in the third gun truck in the middle of a twenty-nine-vehicle supply convoy traveling on Route Tampa between Tikrit and Balad Air Base. Insurgents had turned supply routes in Iraq into shooting galleries where ambushes were common and improvised explosive devices, or IEDs, were hidden in everything from rotting road kill to piles of weeds.

On that day — December 5, 2005 — O'Hara and Willson's unit had spent much of its time at Camp Speicher in Tikrit. The trip south back to Balad should have taken only a few hours. But when a suspicious object thought to be an IED turned up along the route, the convoy sat idle for about two hours while an explosives team determined it a fake.

Real or fake, it was an ominous discovery that set the tone for the rest of the trip. After traveling a short distance south, the convoy approached a highway underpass. On the other side was an Iraqi village. Balad Air Base was only about twenty minutes away.

Tal Afar Mosul
Irbil
Kirkuk
Tikrit
Samarra
Balad
Hilt
Baghdad
Rutbah
Ramadi Fallujah
Karbala
Hillah
Kut
Kufah Diwaniyah
Nasiriyah

Airman First Class Nicole O'Hara receives congratulations from President Bush at Langley Air Force Base in Virginia. Left, Nicole O'Hara stands guard. (Photos courtesy of U.S. Air Force)

"There was a bridge, and we had to pass under it," O'Hara said. "There was a small town there, and as soon as we came under the bridge, the lights went completely out. We knew from intel that was a bad sign."

The convoy had rumbled directly into an ambush.

"I think they were there waiting for us," Willson recalled.

O'Hara agreed.

"We think they staged the fake IED to delay us to give them time to set up," she said. "As soon as the lights went out in the town, the gunfire started."

Airman First Class
Nicole P. O'Hara
U.S. Air Force

- Born July 28, 1984, at Moody Air Force Base in Georgia and raised in Burlington, North Carolina.

- Inducted January 12, 2004. Deployed to the Middle East In 2005, assigned as Airman First Class to 732nd Expeditionary Logistics Readiness Squadron, Detachment 2632, Balad Air Base, Iraq. Also served tour in Saudi Arabia. Later promoted to Senior Airman.

- Both parents are Air Force veterans.

What she did
As a gunner on one of three Humvees protecting a twenty-nine-vehicle convoy, O'Hara and another airman are credited with killing six Iraqi insurgents to defeat an ambush attempt.

Why she joined the Air Force
"I was out of high school for about two years. I was working at IHOP. My dad kept asking me , 'What are you doing with your life?' and I said, 'I don't know.' . . . I had been around the military my whole life, so I thought, 'Why not join?'

Sergeant
Christopher D. Willson
U.S. Air Force

- Born June 10, 1983, in Conway Springs, Kansas.

  - Wife, Chelsie; son, Creighton, three.

  - Inducted in July 2001, first deployed to Middle East in July 2005. At the time of the battle that resulted in his medal, was a staff sergeant assigned to 732nd Expeditionary Logistics Readiness Squadron, Detachment 2632, Balad Air Base, Iraq. Has served six foreign tours of duty in the Middle East, three in Iraq.

What he did
Took the lead in directing a battle to defend a twenty-nine-vehicle convoy that had been ambushed by Iraqi insurgents.

Why he joined the Air Force
"That's a hard question. I joined right out of high school. I wanted to live away from home."

Communicating constantly via radio with his colleagues in the other vehicles, Willson, the assistant convoy commander, knew that one of the trucks had caught fire and that at least one driver had been hit.

As suddenly as it started, the attack was over, and Willson directed all the vehicles to a rallying point about a mile and a half away from the kill zone. He called for medics to fly in from Balad to treat the injured.

Meanwhile, Iraqi fire fighters arrived to extinguish the fire. But there was a glitch — the Iraqis did not speak English, and no one in the convoy spoke Arabic well enough to communicate with them. Willson called back to Balad for a translator.

In the final tally, two civilian convoy personnel were injured and six insurgents were killed.

It still bothers Willson to talk about the chaos and uncertainty of that night.

"I don't like to talk about it, all the fears and what-ifs," he said. "Every time you go out, you expect something to happen to you. You don't know when it's going to happen, you just anticipate it and react to it the best you can with all the training that you have. You never get used to it."

O'Hara has left military life and has struggled emotionally with the events. She and the gunner in truck two, Airman First Class Christian Jackson, were credited with killing the insurgents.

"It was just so awful," she said. "In a situation like that, I had to go get help to realize that it was either us or them and it couldn't be us. It took me a long time to finally accept that." ★

Staff Sergeant Christopher Willson (Photo courtesy of U.S. Air Force)

Nicholas Popaditch

U.S. Marine Corps, Silver Star

By Andrew Lubin

As his M1 Abrams tank, nicknamed Bonecrusher, rolled through Fallujah, Iraq, Gunnery Sergeant Nick Popaditch thought about the trail of dead insurgents left in its wake: "Fight and you die. Run and you die. Hide and you die. Hey, this works for me."

Popaditch, or "Gunny Pop" as his Marines called him, commanded a tank platoon during the first Battle of Fallujah in April 2004. Fighting only a week after four American contractors from Blackwater USA were captured, killed and their bodies hung from a bridge, Bonecrusher and Popaditch's other tank were working with Marine infantry in clearing insurgents out of the city's northwest outskirts.

Popaditch thought that day's fight might be different. Usually the enemy shot a few rocket-propelled grenades and ran; this morning Popaditch heard a higher-than-usual volume of AK-47 fire, along with the deeper bursts of a Russian-made machine gun launching rocket-propelled gre-

Marine Gunnery Sergeant Nick Popaditch, shown in Iraq in 2003. (Photo courtesy of Nick Popaditch)

nades. Maybe this meant the Marines would be engaging a larger force.

Moving into the narrow streets, the commander kept his head on a swivel, looking in every direction as he scanned the rooftops, alleys, doorways, trash drums — anyplace a gunman could hide and shoot Marines advancing through the city.

He spotted a shooter eighty yards away and barked his order: "Gunner — Coax — troops — fire and adjust!" Sitting below him, the gunner loosed a burst of 7.62mm rounds from the coaxial machine gun, killing the gunman.

The Iraqis didn't know that the tanks' arrival had changed the rules of the fight. There would be no more blithely ambushing Marine infantry with RPGs and quick AK-47 bursts from the rooftops.

At night, the Abrams' advanced optics allowed Popaditch to see the enemy long before they could see him. Plus, this same technology let him see through smoke and dust during the day. The coax was fed from a bin holding twenty-eight hundred rounds, and the tank's huge main gun fired a shaped charge that blasted through concrete walls and then exploded.

An Iraqi RPG left only a black mark on the tank's armor that could be wiped off with a wet rag. But an Abrams was a seventy-ton mobile killing machine the likes of which Fallujah had never seen in action.

★★★
189
★★★

As Bonecrusher moved backward to assist an ambushed Marine patrol, small groups of insurgents attacked. It was no contest; Popaditch and his gunner killed them with impunity. Another Marine platoon took station alongside the tank, and together they moved into the city, the infantry ahead of the tank.

"This doesn't work," Popaditch thought. "I can't tell the friendlies from the bad guys."

So in a move that changed Marine urban tank tactics and strategy, he called the infantry platoon leader and suggested a reversed order: The tanks would lead instead of the more vulnerable infantrymen.

The tactic worked. By the end of the first block, the tanks and infantrymen were killing insurgents left and right, and more enemy were rushing forward to stop them. Bonecrusher forced them to fight or run, but they would die either way.

"Engaged and killed six!" the gunner reported. "Engaged and killed four!" Another block into the city: "Engaged and killed three!" The only thing stopping Popaditch's impromptu advance was ammunition, so the Marines ran belts of .50-caliber ammo and some main-gun rounds to him.

The next day, however, Popaditch was not so fortunate. Chasing insurgents down a narrow cross street, he did not see one atop a three-story building fire a rocket-propelled grenade into the tank hatch.

It exploded next to Popaditch's head.

"He put one right in the hatch," Popaditch said. "I knew what had hit me because I heard it right before it hit me. It makes a unique sound, like a snake. I heard, 'Sssss,' then bam! I felt like

Popaditch, "Gunny Pop," takes a break with his tank crew in Iraq. (Photo courtesy of Nick Popaditch)

I got hit in the head with a sledgehammer. I saw a white flash of light like a camera flash, only a lot brighter, and then blackness . . . and all I could hear in my ears was a static."

Still conscious, Popaditch stood inside the tank and tried to assess his injuries as he directed Bonecrusher's crew back to the defensive line. Bleeding badly from the neck and head, he fought to stay awake. Surgeons would later remove what remained of his right eye.

Popaditch's new chapter in Marine urban fighting tactics and his actions to direct his tank crew to safety though badly injured were cited in the commendation that accompanied his Silver Star, which he received November 10, 2005.

But his actions in battle were not extraordinary for a Marine, Popaditch said: "I think every Marine around me would have done the same thing; they just weren't in the same circumstance. And maybe because of where it happened, it was a little more high visibility that somebody wrote a citation for it." ★

Sergeant
Nicholas Popaditch
U.S. Marine Corps

- Born July 2, 1967 in Hammond, Indiana.

- Enlisted in 1986 and served three tours of duty in Iraq, including Desert Storm in 1991 and Operation Iraqi Freedom in 2003.

- Known as "Gunny Pop," Gunnery Sergeant. Popaditch served in 2nd Battalion, 1st Marines.

- Has written a book, *Once a Marine*, about his military service and recovery from his injuries.

What he did

On the battlefield, Popaditch suggested and implemented a new and reverse urban fighting method by putting tanks in front of infantry. A day later, he was severely wounded when a rocket-propelled grenade exploded next to his head. Still, he managed the safe return of his tank and crew.

Why he joined the Marines

"I was going nowhere with my life when a recruiter called me up. It all sounded good. He was telling me all the things you could do in the Marine Corps, and he was talking about teamwork in everything you do, and I was thinking, 'This all sounds great.' "

Popaditch strikes a pose in his "dress blues" at the 2004 Marine Corps Ball. (Photo courtesy of Nick Popaditch)

Tal Afar

Tikrit

Samarra
Balad

Hilt

Baghdad
Ramadi Fallujah

Karbala
Hillah
Kut

Kufah Diwaniyah

Nasiriyah

Basra

Clayton M. Rankin

Colorado Army National Guard, Bronze Star with Valor

By Kris Antonelli

CLAY RANKIN, A POLICE OFFICER IN SUBURBAN DENVER, knew what it was like to kill even before he was sent to the Middle East in the first Gulf War. He and a fellow officer fatally shot a man who had taken a pharmacy clerk hostage in 1990.

But a year later, the military police officer returned to his job as a civilian police officer with the Northglenn, Colorado, Police Department with grim scenes of burning oil fields and charred bodies stuck in his mind. Old haunts, familiar streets and routine police work were distorted by the memories of war. He had nightmares, anxiety and flashbacks. He un-holstered his gun during routine traffic stops. One night, while sitting in his cruiser in a parking lot and completing paperwork, he heard a noise behind him.

"I opened the door, rolled out on my stomach and took my gun out," Rankin said. "It was a just a kid walking across the parking lot."

The department's psychologist diagnosed him with Post Traumatic Stress Disorder. Rankin didn't believe it. His symptoms had to be a reaction to the toxin gases he was exposed to during his tour.

"I just chalked it all up — the nightmares, the flashbacks, my over-reactions — to the change, because you never come back the same," he said.

Although the police chief tried to find an assignment that would take Rankin off the street, it was not possible in a small agency such as Northglenn's. He had no choice but to retire.

Finally, in 1995, his marriage and family life strained by his recurring symptoms, he went to a veterans hospital looking specifically for PTSD treatment. In therapy, he learned techniques to manage his symptoms. His health and personal life improved. He started a private investigation business, which became successful.

But at the start of the second Gulf War, Rankin's passion for law enforcement led him to join the National Guard as a military police officer. He believed he was well enough to handle redeploying with his old unit to Iraq.

He landed at Camp Udairi, in northern Kuwait at the Iraqi border, just as the ground war began. Standing in line at the PX in March 2003, Rankin waited to get supplies needed to push north when a terrorist in a white pick-up truck plowed through the line.

"Everybody started running for cover except for me," he said. "I spun around and got in front of the vehicle to pull him away from the soldiers and towards me. He was coming toward me. I was drawing my pistol, loading my clip and chambering a round and preparing to fire. I couldn't fire on him right away because of the soldiers who were behind him, so I had to wait. He was probably five feet from me and coming at me, and I shot him and kind of dove out of the way and cracked my skull on the ground."

Rankin doesn't remember many details that followed, but his colleagues said he chased down the truck as it was coming to a stop, shot the driver twice more and pulled him out.

A month later, Rankin's unit was escorting military officials around Fallujah. As he was loading a two hundred fifty-pound

★★★
192
★★★

Clay Rankin and his specially trained dog, Archie, take a break from an Army Wounded Warrior Program training seminar in Washington, D.C. Archie, a Labrador Retriever, was donated to Rankin by the nonprofit group Patriot Paws, which matches disabled veterans with dogs trained to help them manage daily life. (Photo courtesy of Clay Rankin)

Mk-19 grenade launcher on the turret of a truck, he slipped, hitting his head on the turret before landing on his back on a rock on the ground. According to witnesses, he got back up, hoisted the Mk-19 on the truck and finished the mission.

"It's not like there was a doctor around the corner," Rankin recalled. "Unless you lost an arm or a leg, you just didn't run to the doctor. All I knew is that the pain kept getting worse in my body."

And that's when he started doing what he calls "the crazy stuff."

Rankin cleared dangerous buildings by himself instead of getting help from fellow soldiers. He played chicken with vehicles on Route Tampa, the main north-south highway, by standing in the middle of the road and pointing his pistol.

"I would have shot them if they didn't stop," he said.

Sergeant Clay Rankin in Iraq. (Photo courtesy of Clay Rankin.)

Rankin's superiors sent him to a psychiatrist at a nearby airbase. For the second time, Rankin was diagnosed with PTSD — but this time the doctor said it was "acute." He was sent home and again went to the veterans administration for help.

SERGEANT
Clayton M. Rankin
Colorado Army National Guard

- Born in 1961 in the Denver area.

- Married twenty-five years; three children.

- Joined the Army in 1979 as a military police officer and stayed until 1982. Volunteered as a Reservist — 220th Military Police Company, Colorado National Guard — and first deployed to Saudi Arabia and Kuwait in 1990. Deployed with the same unit to Iraq in 2003.

- Retired as an MP sergeant, he lives in West Virginia and works as an advocate with the Army Wounded Warrior Program, helping veterans readjust to civilian life.

What he did
Credited with saving 300 lives by shooting a terrorist who plowed through a commissary in a vehicle.

Why he joined the military
"All I have ever wanted to do was serve my country and my community. Despite my injuries and everything that has happened, I wouldn't change a thing. I would do it all over again."

He was among the thousands of vets who returned home from Iraq or Afghanistan with post-traumatic stress. Although he received a Bronze Star with Valor for his actions at Camp Udairi and is credited with saving 300 lives in that terrorist attack, facing up to his illness and learning to manage it could be considered his most heroic act.

And he struggled with coming to grips with his service and medal.

"You know what's crazy about all of this is that they never gave me a medal for saving people's lives, but they sure gave them to me for taking someone's life," he said. "Of course they claimed that I saved 300 lives, but I don't buy that."

He had biofeedback therapy, a technique that taught him how his body responds to stress and how to control his breathing and heart rate in situations that stress him. And he agreed to take medication for depression, stress and anxiety.

He also decided he needed a total change in environment and moved his family to West Virginia, where there were fewer stress triggers.

Two years ago Rankin met Archie, a black Labrador retriever trained to help him with everyday mobility

issues that stem from the back injury when he fell off the truck in Iraq. Archie also knows how to calm Rankin when a flashback sets in and can rouse him from nightmares.

"You manage PTSD, you never get over it," he said. "But I am OK with that. I have learned how to manage it and how to create an environment where I can function and even thrive."

★ ★★★

195

★★★

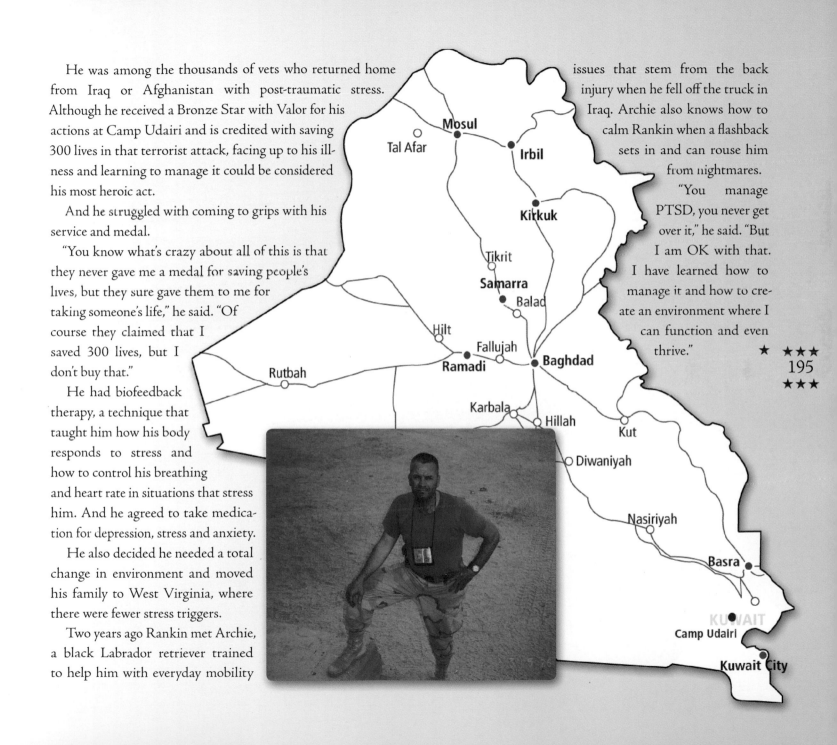

Alvin E. Shell Jr.

U.S. Army, Bronze Star with Valor

By Ellen N. Woods

(Photo courtesy of Alvin Shell)

FIRST HE FELT THE HEAT FROM THE ROCKET-PROPELLED grenade as it flew over his shoulder. Then the force of the RPG blew him off the road and into a ditch, knocking him out for about thirty seconds. As First Lieutenant Alvin Shell staggered out of the ditch, the pitch-black night was now illuminated by an inferno.

The grenade's sparks had ignited the diesel fuel spilling from an eighteen-wheeler that had been hit by a roadside bomb and was clogging traffic on the busy supply route outside Baghdad.

"I could see people running around on fire, screaming," Shell recalled. "The fire was racing down the road, chasing the gasoline."

Shell and his platoon from the 21st Military Police/Airborne had come to the aid of a disabled American convoy.

And now they were the ones who needed help.

Platoon Sergeant Wesley Spaid was engulfed in flames and screaming for help.

"I ran up the road as the fire was coming toward me," Shell remembered. "I ran through it and got to him. I tried to pat him out. I threw dirt on him. I hugged him. I rolled on him — anything to get the fire out. But he was covered in gasoline."

Shell didn't give up, finally extinguishing the fire and directing his sergeant out of the flames. But as he turned to look for others to help, the wall of fire grew around him. There was no way out.

Soaked in gasoline himself, Shell grabbed his rifle with one hand, covered his face with the other, and ran into the flames.

"I lit up like a Christmas tree," Shell said.

He ran frantically from truck to truck looking for a fire extinguisher but then remembered that they had been used during a recent engagement. He pulled off his armored vest and shirt and saw that his skin was on fire.

Desperate, Shell jumped into the same ditch he had emerged from only minutes earlier. He frantically rolled around, covering himself with parasite-infested dirt and water. Finally, the flames were out.

Shell began to look for his rifle. Still in charge, he asked for a count of all weapons and soldiers and was assured that everyone had made it. The platoon decided to drive back to Camp Victory rather than wait for helicopters to ferry the injured. For two more miles, Shell remained the officer in charge.

Arriving at Camp Victory, he got out of his vehicle but collapsed as he tried to stand up, his soldiers catching him before he hit the ground. He remembers getting morphine for the pain and being loaded onto the helicopter.

His captain saw him off and said he was a hero.

In response, Shell joked: "I'm not a hero. A hero is a sandwich. I'm a paratrooper."

He doesn't remember much about the next few days, not the medevac helicopter ride or the transport to Landstuhl Regional Medical Center in Germany, where he was stabilized.

Since he had been placed in a life-saving, medically induced coma, Shell also doesn't remember the Army surgical team that flew from Brooke Army Medical Center in San Antonio to escort him back to its burn unit.

When he opened his eyes four days later, he clearly remembers seeing his wife at his bedside and his father standing behind her.

"I was infuriated," he said. "I couldn't believe the Army had flown my wife and dad to Iraq. What were they thinking?"

Shell thought just a few hours had passed since the attack. He didn't know he was in Texas. He was in and out of consciousness and has only the few memories.

He does remember his wife Danielle pulling her surgical mask down and leaning over him. He remembers the kiss. He also remembers indescribable pain.

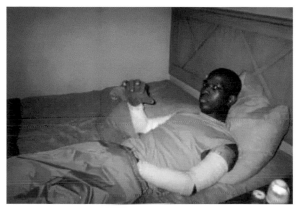

During the early stages of Alvin Shell's recovery, his wounds were bandaged as they healed and as his grafted skin became viable. "Patients with severe battlefield burns are surviving at rates we have never seen before," says Lieutenant Colonel Evan Renz, the surgeon in charge of the Burn Unit at Brooke Army Medical Center at Fort Sam Houston. "Advances in medical care and rapid evacuation have made a difference. Within hours of his injuries, Captain Shell was in an operating room at a Level I trauma center, and all of his burns were excised and grafted. And within three days, he was here at the burn center receiving state-of-the-art burn care. That is the key to survival. In the Vietnam era, it would have taken fourteen to eighteen days." (Photo courtesy of Alvin Shell)

"I kept asking my dad where my weapon was," he said. "That was my major concern for a few days. My dad was a sport. He kept telling me, 'We'll find it.' It really took a few days to realize the extent of my injuries and how my life had changed."

Shell had been deployed for ten months in Iraq. He wasn't supposed to be on patrol the night of August 31, 2004, when his world erupted in flames. But he had volunteered to cover for another lieutenant who had made a scheduling error and went out that night in charge of her platoon.

Shell liked patrol. His brigade was stationed at Camp Victory, in the area surrounding the Baghdad International Airport, after coming off a four-month assignment in Fallujah, site of some of the war's fiercest battles.

The mission at Camp Victory was to run patrols in and around Baghdad. Often that included providing convoy escorts.

The soldiers enjoyed interacting with the Iraqi public. They believed they were winning hearts and minds with soccer balls, crayons, pencils, candy and T-shirts. Shell "adopted" a family who lived on a trash dump, bringing them food, school supplies and care packages his family sent from the United States.

★★★
197
★★★

Danielle was living at Fort Bragg, North Carolina, with the family's three children. The horrible news came while the baby, Jachin, was napping and her two older boys, Sean and Trey, were at school. The phone rang, and when she heard the voice of her husband's captain, she knew immediately that the news was bad.

Since she didn't know if she would be flown to Germany or wait until Alvin arrived stateside, she began mobilizing her family so she could leave on a moment's notice. Her dad would come to North Carolina to stay with the older boys, while her mom would take the baby. Shell's parents were preparing to leave with Danielle.

The rush of activity in the Shell home has been played out in countless military homes during the Iraq and Afghanistan wars. As of mid-October, 2009, 4,302 service members have been wounded in action in Afghanistan, 31,529 in Iraq.

Brooke Army Medical Center received many of the most seriously injured, with 4,326 soldiers, Marines, sailors and airmen checking in for recovery and rehabilitation as of August 2009. Besides Shell, the Institutes of Surgical Research Burn Center at Brooke has treated 786 other service members with combat burns.

When Danielle first arrived at the medical center, she remembers feeling relief. "He's here, he's in one piece," she said. "Everything else we can handle."

She didn't know that the road ahead would include eighteen months at the hospital, thirty surgeries, including painful skin grafts, and countless hours of physical therapy.

When Shell woke up, he could move only his left arm.

"I went from being a paratrooper going one hundred miles an hour to not being able to feed myself," he said. "My face and body had swollen up. I couldn't even move my head."

As Alvin Shell began his long road to recovery at Brooke Army Medical Center (BAMC) at Fort Sam Houston in San Antonio, his family challenged him to learn to walk again before his baby Jachin took his first steps. (Photo courtesy of Alvin Shell)

Because Shell had shielded his face as he raced through the flames, his injuries are not always apparent at first glance. He had third-degree burns over 33 percent of his body. Major muscle groups on his right side actually burned off. He lost parts of his hamstring, his quadriceps, his calf and his biceps. He was burned to the bone on several parts of his arm, leg and hand.

Such significant burns mean that a patient can't control his body temperature or loss of fluids from the body, which can lead to infection. Vital organs and the nervous system also can be affected, doctors say.

While Shell was in critical condition, Danielle and her father-in-law moved to San Antonio, arriving at the Burn Unit ICU

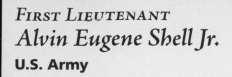

FIRST LIEUTENANT
Alvin Eugene Shell Jr.
U.S. Army

- Born December 17, 1976, in Virginia Beach, Virginia.

- Wife Danielle; sons Sean, Trey and Jachin.

- Joined Army in September 2000 and deployed to Iraq in January 2004 with the 21st Military Police Company (Airborne) of the 16th Military Police Brigade (Airborne). Medically retired with the rank of captain.

What he did

Ran through fire, saving a sergeant from being consumed by flames. Suffered third-degree burns over a third of his body and underwent thirty surgeries over eighteen months.

Why he joined the Army

"I had student loans, and the Army had a good program for student loan repayment. My wife was an Army brat — both of her parents were active duty. And my dad had served in the Army during the Vietnam era. My wife really thought I would do well in the Army. She was right. It was a good fit."

Before he was injured, Shell enjoyed frequent interactions with Iraqi families, sharing food, school supplies, and care packages send from home. (Photo courtesy Alvin Shell)

199

Tal Afar
Mosul
Irbil
Kirkuk
Tikrit
Samarra
Balad
Hilt
Ramadi Fallujah
Baghdad
Karbala
Hillah
Kut
Kufah
Diwaniyah
Nasiriyah
Basra

every morning at six to feed Shell breakfast and staying until after dinner. As he stabilized, Danielle returned to North Carolina to see her older boys, bring Jachin back with her and enroll him in daycare at Fort Sam Houston.

The family also issued a challenge to Shell: He had to walk again before Jachin took his first steps.

"It was really difficult to stand up," Shell said. "My body was shrinking up from atrophy, and I didn't have many muscles left on my right side. It was training the muscle that was left to work again. I was literally putting my arms around physical therapists and learning to stand up and take one step at a time. It was a slow progression."

Grafted skin must be stressed for hours a day if is to become pliable and functional.

"You constantly have to move the skin at all of your joints or it will harden and lock you up," Shell said. "Sometimes in physical therapy, as I would straighten my arm, the skin would actually rip open and I would need another graft. It wasn't pretty."

Lieutenant Colonel Evan Renz, the surgeon in charge of the burn unit, said that when the full thickness of skin is destroyed in third-degree burns, all of the nerves that live in the skin are destroyed. When new skin is grafted, a whole new neural

Alvin Shell's winning smile and untouched face offer no clue to severity of his injuries sustained during an insurgent attack in Baghdad in August 2004. When he is wearing short sleeves or shorts, the scarring from multiple skin grafts to the right side of his body are apparent. Often, he says, it is children who feel most comfortable asking what happened to him. (Photo courtesy of Alvin Shell)

network must re-grow, and this can cause "horrendous pain."

"We all remember Captain Shell," Renz said. "His positive outlook was remarkable. He was focused forward. Through all of that pain, I can't recall him ever complaining."

Shell credits the medical staff: "The doctors, the nurses, the physical therapists, all the specialists — they pieced me back together. And it took a long time."

The older boys moved to Texas a few months later, and the family moved into a unit at Fisher House, which provides housing to families of the seriously injured. Eventually, Shell joined his family at its temporary quarters and continued his rehabilitation as an outpatient.

And he won the family's challenge to walk before Jachin.

Shell said he came back through his family: "All the scars you see on the outside don't come close to the scars I have on the inside. . . . The healing process was the will to keep going. To go through fifteen surgeries, knowing you have fifteen more — that will came from my family. There is no way I could have kept going without them."

He also was inspired by other wounded warriors he met at Brooke and by one young soldier in particular.

"I was in excruciating pain," Shell explained. "The pain in my leg was unbearable. I felt like I couldn't do it any more. I was done. I wasn't doing any more physical therapy. I was complaining, and this kid, maybe nineteen years old, told me he wished he had a leg. And I look over, and he didn't have a leg. And I felt so terrible. He told me, 'For the time you can't run, don't worry about it. But for the times that you can run, run. For the times you can walk, walk straight. Give it 100 percent.' And that's what I do."

Shell was awarded a Purple Heart and the Bronze Star with Valor for his heroism in saving Sergeant Spaid. The biggest honor, however, came when the presentation was delayed until his brigade came home, allowing him to receive the awards alongside the soldiers who had fought with him.

"Awards are given," he said. "Respect is earned."

Danielle doesn't like that her husband downplays the award for heroism: "The reality is that not everyone would have done what Alvin did. And if he hadn't, Sergeant Spaid's children might not have their dad."

Today, Shell and his family live in Virginia. He is medically retired from the Army as a captain and works for the Department of Homeland Security. And he recently graduated from the FBI National Academy.

He is active with the Army's Wounded Warrior Program, which provides assistance and advocacy for wounded soldiers and their families from the time they are injured throughout their lives. The program has helped Shell navigate the maze of medical and disability benefits and find his way as a medically retired soldier. He serves as a spokesman when asked. It isn't always easy to relive the events of that night, but he does it out of duty.

Shell said he is mentally stronger than before he was injured: "Sometimes you have to experience the bad to appreciate all the good in your life."

Still, he lives in chronic pain. He can't grip a football or basketball because he has limited range of motion in his right hand. That's something he wishes he could do with his boys.

For the most part, however, he lives without regret.

"There are still nights my wife holds me a little tighter than others," Shell said. "To be honest, I don't want the dreams to go away. It would be an injustice to those who were involved, those who didn't make it. It's who I am. I don't want to get over it." ★

★★★
201
★★★

Alvin Shell lives in Virginia with wife Danielle and their three sons, from left in front row, Sean, Jachin and Trey. (Photo courtesy of Alvin Shell)

(Photo courtesy of John Vanlandingham)

John F. Vanlandingham

Arkansas National Guard, Silver Star

By Lewis Delavan

BULLETS, GRENADES, SHRAPNEL AND SMOKE SEARED THE desert. Danger lurked where reed-lined ditches hid ambushers on the narrow, isolated dirt road.

"You couldn't see anything from the dust and the smoke as we moved through the explosive area," Captain John Vanlandingham recalls. "I saw a black object coming through the air over the reeds. It landed about five feet from me in a tire rut. Luckily, it rolled away. I dove down by a wounded soldier and the grenade blew."

It was November 14, 2004, and the insurgency was rocking the Sunni Triangle. Leader of a ten-vehicle convoy that came under attack, the thirty-seven-year-old Arkansas Army National Guard captain from tiny New Blaine, ninety-seven miles northwest of Little Rock, refused to leave behind the Iraqis he had trained to become guardsmen.

Twenty miles short of safety at Camp Taji, north of Baghdad, blasts from improvised explosive devices (IEDs) ripped motors, trucks and human bodies during the enemy attack.

One explosion pitched twenty-five Iraqis from an unarmed troop carrier into a ditch. Three dead and others wounded. None, however, would be left behind.

Smoke hid the carnage. Some two hundred yards toward safety, Vanlandingham realized one Iraqi vehicle was missing. He told his sergeant to reverse the Humvee and ordered a Mark-19 grenade launcher to cover one roadside, two 50-caliber machine guns to cover the other.

Vanlandingham then ran into the kill zone.

The first Iraqi was small. "I just scooped him up," Vanlandingham said of pulling the victim from the three-foot-deep ditch. The captain re-entered heavy fire and returned to his Humvee, fifty feet away.

He ran to another victim.

"He was a lot bigger. I could tell I wasn't going to move him," Vanlandingham said. "I yelled at an Iraqi close by to help move the wounded soldier."

Pain seared Vanlandingham's back as the pair hoisted the victim from the ditch. A ruptured disk and pain remain to this day.

The Iraqis whom he trained had performed well conducting raids, controlling traffic, preparing to protect their homes.

But trapped in the ditch, many shot wildly; some fired into the air. Others sat crying, numbed by shock.

Vanlandingham repeatedly entered the kill zone to pull out wounded and dead Iraqis, direct the able-bodied to safety and recover weapons.

Ready to depart after recovering the last body from the ditch, the bloodied and weary captain realized he had not checked the crippled truck.

"We had just started to move when an Iraqi in the Leland raised his hand," he said. "We were about to leave him."

The soldier was missing a leg. "His leg was a couple of feet from my face," he said. "I saw that (another) man was dead.

"It was probably a one hundred-foot run with this (wounded) guy," he said. "I threw him into the back of the Humvee."

Vanlandingham returned to recover the body of the dead man — one last time into the battle zone.

★ ★ ★

203

★ ★ ★

All told, the captain saved about a dozen Iraqis that day. The insurgents eventually would have returned and killed the wounded, he said.

Vanlandingham didn't hesitate to act. It was his duty, he said. It was his training.

His heroics earned him the Silver Star.

"God had his hands on me that day," he said. "I don't know how I wasn't hit." ★

Captain John Vanlandingham earned a Silver Star for his heroism in Iraq in 2004. Below, Vanlandingham, a member of the Arkansas National Guard, stands near a display commemorating his valor in Iraq. (Photos courtesy of John Vanlandingham)

Captain
John F. Vanlandingham
Arkansas National Guard

- Born March 30, 1967, in Clinton, Wisconsin. Family moved to Paris, Arkansas, when he was fifteen.

- Married to Lisa for ten years.

- Resident of New Blaine, Arkansas. Graduated in 1985 from Paris High School. Attended Southern Arkansas University-Camden on a basketball scholarship. Graduated from Henderson State University with a graphics design degree.

- Joined Air Force in 1992 and served five years. Joined Arkansas Army National Guard. Completed Officer's Candidate School at Camp Robinson, Arkansas, and commissioned in 1999.

- Assigned to Arkansas Army National Guard, 39th Infantry Brigade combat team, First battalion. Served from March 2004 to March 2005.

What he did
Saved the lives of twelve Iraqis whom he had trained to become guardsmen when their convoy came under heavy attack in the Sunni Triangle.

Why he joined the Army
"People don't know how good they have it here. We're so much better off over here."

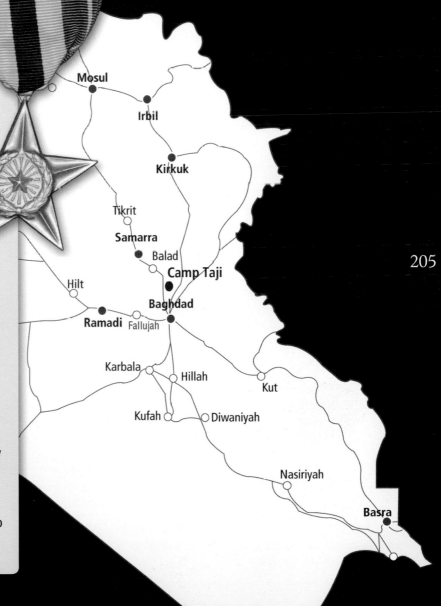

Christopher B. Waiters

U.S. Army, Distinguished Service Cross

By S.L. Alligood

AS HE RACED TOWARD THE BURNING TANK, THE WHIZ-zing sounds of small arms fire speeding past his head, Specialist Christopher Waiters never thought twice about the risks.

"You start thinking about life," he said, "but it's already too late for that. So you just keep going."

An insurgent's bomb had exploded beneath the Bradley Fighting Vehicle, spewing a black stream of smoke into the skies of Baqubah, Iraq, where Waiters' unit had been on patrol the morning of April 5, 2007.

"My group was cleaning a real bad neighborhood. They were blowing a lot of American soldiers up in that area," recalled Waiters, a medic with the 2nd Infantry Division, 3rd Stryker Brigade Combat Team, 5th Battalion, 20th Infantry Regiment.

His unit had patrolled for more than twenty-four hours when the explosion shook the ground.

Waiters knew what he had to do: "I dismounted of my own accord and ran through enemy fire and started pulling people out of the tank."

The soldier, then twenty-five, fired his M-4 at two insurgents as he ran the 100 yards to the Bradley, now belching flame. Other enemies he couldn't see were all around.

It was the worst possible situation for the Americans, under fire from rooftops and alleyways at a marketplace where a couple of hundred people were now scrambling to get out of the way.

And the street was filled with other vehicles. Was one rigged with a second bomb?

Arriving at the Bradley, Waiters had two other worries: the intense heat from the flames and a cache of 25mm ammunition that was beginning to "cook off" inside the demolished tank. He knew he didn't want to be around when rounds started exploding.

Waiters clambered aboard the Bradley, grabbed the driver and gunner and led them to safety. Then he returned to the burning tank to rescue a third soldier. That soldier, unfortunately, was dead, killed by the bomb blast beneath his feet.

Waiters was unhurt during the rescue, though parts of his uniform and combat boots melted from the fire's intense heat.

And today he speaks somewhat fatalistically about the whole event: "I guess when you're put into a situation like that, you're either going to get it or not. It's rolling the dice."

Waiters believes the two Fort Hood, Texas, soldiers whom he pulled from the Bradley survived their burns and wounds. He regrets being unable to help the third soldier.

For his bravery, Waiters received the Distinguished Service Cross, the Army's second-highest military decoration, awarded for "extreme gallantry and risk of life in actual combat."

Waiters never expected to receive a medal, much less such a prestigious award.

"When they told me I had been put in for a Distinguished Service Cross, I had to actually go and look it up because I had never seen one before," he said.

Later promoted to staff sergeant, Waiters now trains a new generation of medics. His message to them is simple:

"Take (the job) seriously and pay attention to detail. Be proud of what you do and don't take it lightly." ★

Specialist Christopher Waiters makes his first attempt to climb into a Bradley Infantry Fighting Vehicle that had caught fire with soldiers inside. Waiters knew he was putting his life on the line. "I guess when you're put into a situation like that, you're either going to get it or not," he said. "It's rolling the dice."

Army Vice Chief of Staff General Peter Chiarelli presents the Distinguished Service Cross to Christopher Waiters during an October 23, 2008, ceremony at Fort Lewis, Washington. Waiters, a specialist at the time of the incident, was a staff sergeant when he received his award. (U.S. Army photo)

SPECIALIST
Christopher B. Waiters
U.S. Army

* Born March 13, 1982 in Landstuhl, Germany. Grew up in Germany and Seattle.

* Nickname is Doc.

* Wife, Susan; daughter, Ryanna, six. Father, Bernard Waiters Jr., served in Operation Desert Storm.

• Joined the Army in 1999 and has served two tours in Iraq.

What he did
Pulled three soldiers from a burning tank while under fire from insurgents.

Why he joined the Army
"I had nothing better to do. College was too expensive. I'll never get out. I'll die in this uniform."

Benjamin West
U.S. Army, Bronze Star with Valor

By Kevin Maurer

Benjamin West of Tempe, Arizona, an infantryman with D Company, 2nd Battalion, 325th Airborne Infantry Regiment, 82nd Airborne Division, fits a piece of colored cloth embroidered with the Star of David into the flap of his body armor. West carries the cloth, which was sent to him by his aunt, with him on all his patrols. (US Army photo by Sergeant Mike Pryor, 2nd BCT Public Affairs)

FROM THE GUN TURRET OF HIS ARMORED HUMVEE, Specialist Ben West scanned the windows and roofs in central Baghdad, searching for any sign of a gunman or sniper. Suddenly, he saw a flash and a smoke trail and heard someone yell, "RPG!"

Seconds later, a rocket-propelled grenade skipped off the hood of the Humvee and hit the turret, showering West with shrapnel. The force of the blast sent him down into the turret.

The 82nd's Airborne Division's 2nd Brigade Combat Team had moved into Baghdad in 2007 as part of a new U.S. strategy in Iraq. It was hoped that an increase of 21,500 troops would bring the chaos in the capital under control. In May, West's unit was in Sadr City, the infamous Shiia slum.

When they were attacked, the paratroopers were putting up Hesco barriers — head-high mesh baskets filled with dirt — to fortify a joint security station in the neighborhood.

After the blast, all West could see was red dust. For a second, he thought he was dead and in hell. But the screams of the driver, Private First Class Thomas Ponce, brought him back to reality.

"I needed to get out of the vehicle and needed to get him out of the vehicle," West recalled.

Throwing open the passenger-side door, he ran through a maelstrom of fire to the driver's side and helped Ponce out, dragging him to safety and the medics who could treat his broken arm and shrapnel wounds.

West returned to the truck, climbing back into the turret to begin firing the .50-caliber machine gun.

"They had just blown up my truck," West explained. "They were the enemy, and you want to fire back at them.

"The .50 cal is the most casualty-producing weapon. Once you start hearing that and there are rounds coming at you, you are not going to stay and fight."

West's unit mates finally pulled him off the truck. The fire was igniting ammunition, and his arms and legs were covered with shrapnel wounds.

"He refused medical attention," said Leigh Kennedy, his platoon leader at the time. "We got behind cover and started returning fire. He just kept on being a perfect soldier."

West kept fighting until the medevac arrived. He and Ponce were rushed to the hospital in Baghdad's Green Zone. He spent a few weeks recovering before returning to his unit and finishing his deployment.

★★★
210
★★★

Kennedy said he was in awe when he saw West pull Ponce to safety: "This is what you dream about. You hope a soldier will step up and do something like that. It was amazing to watch. He showed so much selfless service, so much courage. It changed the whole course of the incident."

Kennedy recommended West for a medal.

"He did above and beyond what he was supposed to do," Kennedy said. "You train your soldiers, but there are some things that soldiers do more than you train to do. That is a privilege."★

Specialist
Benjamin West
U.S. Army

- Born: August 9, 1985, in Seattle, Washington.

- Single.

- Assigned to 2nd Battalion, 325th Airborne Infantry Regiment. Deployed three times to Iraq.

What he did
Ignoring his own shrapnel wounds, he rescued the injured driver of his Humvee, then climbed back into the burning vehicle to return enemy fire.

Why he joined the Army
"It was something I always wanted to do. It was a civic duty. It was something I should do to give back to the country."

Major General David Rodriguez, commander of the 82nd Airborne Division presented Specialist Ben West with a Bronze Star with V device at a Fort Bragg, North Carolina ceremony. West saved his driver from a flaming Humvee despite also being wounded in a rocket propelled grenade attack.

Jeremiah W. Workman

U.S. Marine Corps, Navy Cross

By James C. Roberts

AS HE LAY EXHAUSTED AND BARELY CONSCIOUS ON THE blood-soaked stone floor of a Fallujah house, his lungs begging for oxygen that had been sucked out by a grenade's concussion, Corporal Jeremiah Workman thought the end was near.

"I felt like I was in a dream," Workman recalled. "The last of my strength was draining away. I tried to get up but fell face down in the broken glass on the floor. My arms and hands were covered with blood. I thought I was dying. It just got black, and I thought that was death."

As he was drifting off, Workman was awakened by the voice of Major Todd Desgrosseilliers, the battalion executive officer, who was dragging him to safety. "Let's go, Marine!" Desgrosseilliers shouted. "We're getting out NOW!"

The date was December 23, 2004. Just hours earlier, Workman's unit, Mortar Platoon, Weapons Company, 5th Marine Regiment, 3rd Battalion, was mopping up, searching for weapons caches and booby traps in a Fallujah neighborhood after U.S. forces had subdued insurgents in Operation Phantom Fury, the second Battle of Fallujah.

Suddenly, shots rang out from a house across the street, and gray and white smoke of gunfire poured from windows on the second floor. Five Marines from Workman's platoon had entered a house defended by an estimated forty heavily armed insurgents. Badly outnumbered, the Marines were trapped.

"I said, 'We gotta go get those guys,'" Workman said.

Workman and seven others in the squad entered the house and were met by a hail of bullets from the second floor. "The wall behind the staircase was just about falling apart from all the bullets that were shooting around," he said.

Making his way up the staircase, Workman spied the trapped Marines but had to retreat back down. Trying again, the would-be rescuers advanced up the stairs.

"We fought back and forth," Workman recalled. "There was a lot of firepower coming out of the bedrooms." Then a grenade bounced out of a bedroom and toward the Marines.

CORPORAL
Jeremiah W. Workman

U.S. Marine Corps

- Born August 26, 1983, in Marion, Ohio.

- Wife, Jessica; son, Devon, two.

- Joined the Marines on August 28, 2000, and deployed to Iraq on September 10, 2004. Was assigned to Mortar Platoon, Weapons Company, 3rd Battalion, 5th Marine Regiment, Regimental Combat team one, 1st Marine Division.

What he did

Repeatedly charged into a house where insurgents had trapped men from his unit. Battled for three hours to rescue the Marines, carrying one to safety despite his own injuries.

Why he joined the Marines

"My sophomore or junior year sitting in the cafeteria at school and I saw the Marine recruiters come in for the first time. You can tell when those guys come in, everyone stops what they are doing. I was just mesmerized. Each time they came back I would pay attention. It was the way they walked, the way they carried themselves, the way they talked . . . it was impressive to me."

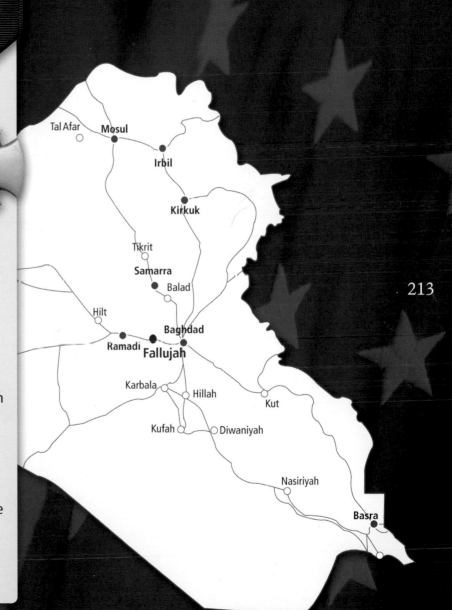

Workman raised his leg to shield himself. "I remember there was a lot of flame that lit the room," he said. "I felt like someone hit me in the leg with a ball bat. I heard guys yell. They had been hit."

Though peppered with shrapnel, the Marines kept fighting until they ran out of ammunition and had to leave the house, again under heavy fire.

"Marines were running back to get ammo," Workman said. "That's when I saw one Marine stagger out of the neighboring yard. He looked a zombie, covered with blood. He fell to his knees and just fell over." The Marine had jumped out of the house.

Workman pulled the man on his back and half-carried, half-dragged him out of the yard, evading sniper fire richocheting off the sidewalk.

"I dragged him about seventy-five yards," Workman said, "but it felt like two hundred miles. I was already dehydrated. I was just hurting."

Workman wrote afterward that his stomach felt "like I've got the worst case of the flu imaginable. We've been fighting for over two hours in hundred-plus heat, running and fighting, getting grenaded and suffering from smoke inhalation. I've never felt this level of complete fatigue, utter exhaustion."

At the casualty collection point, Workman spied two dead Marines lying in the back of a vehicle, one of them from his squad. It was the first time he had seen a dead Marine.

"It was like someone flipped a switch on me. I went into a rage," Workman said. "I wanted to kill every insurgent in the house."

Workman receives the Paul Ray Smith Award at a 2007 ceremony. With him is Carlton Kent, Sergeant Major of the Marine Corps. (Photo courtesy of American Veterans Center)

Workman and three others rushed the house a third time. Again they were met with a slam of automatic weapons fire, and this time three of the insurgents charged into the Marines. The jihadists were repelled, peppered with rifle fire.

But out of the smoke came yet another grenade, which knocked Workman down. Exhausted, dazed and dehydrated, Workman thought his days were done until Desgrosseilliers shook him and pulled him up.

"He grabbed me by my Kevlar, 'cause I really couldn't move," Workman said. I was puking all over — you know, blood — because I was so dehydrated. He grabbed me by my helmet and dragged me out of the house."

Two of the trapped Marines were killed in the fight. Their bodies were dropped out of the house by Marines who escaped by jumping out after them. A third Marine, from Workman's unit, also was killed.

With the Marines evacuated, an arriving M1 tank finally blasted the second floor of the house, and aerial bombs finished leveling the building.

Workman's actions that day contributed to the killing of twenty-four insurgents and the rescue of the survivors, the Marine Corps said when it awarded him the Navy Cross, its second-highest award for combat valor.

He has since written a book, *Shadow of the Sword*, recounting the fight and his battles with Post-Traumatic Stress Disorder in the years that have followed. ★

Corporal Workman is presented with his Navy Cross by Brigadier General Richard T. Tryon, commanding general of Marine Corps Recruit Depot, Parris Island, South Carolina, in May 2006. (Photo by Troy Loveless)

CONTRIBUTORS

S.L. Alligood was a reporter for nearly thirty years before joining Middle Tennessee State University as an assistant professor in journalism in August 2008. Alligood worked at weekly newspapers before being hired by the daily newspapers in Nashville. He was a general assignment reporter, an environment reporter, a columnist and a war correspondent, with assignments in Afghanistan and Iraq as an embedded reporter with the 101st Airborne Division.

Kris Antonelli is a freelance journalist based in the Baltimore-Washington area whose work focuses on counterterrorism and the military. While a student at Johns Hopkins University Zanvyl Krieger School of Arts and Sciences, she traveled to Israel and the occupied territories to complete her graduate non-fiction writing project. Her articles have appeared in *Baltimore* magazine, the *Washington Post*, several local publications and secured federal government Web sites. Previously, as a staff writer at the *Baltimore Sun*, she covered the U.S. Naval Academy, law enforcement and politics.

David Briscoe served thirty-nine years with The Associated Press after a stint in the Peace Corps as an English teacher in the Philippines. He led AP coverage of Utah and Idaho in the 1970s as Intermountain news editor, the Philippines in the 1980s as Manila bureau chief and Washington in the 1990s as international desk supervisor. He then headed the Honolulu Bureau, retiring from AP in 2009. He is now an independent journalist and editor of *MediaLine* newsletter for the East-West Center in Honolulu.

Thomas L. Day is a military writer for the McClatchy Company and *The* (Macon, Georgia.) *Telegraph*. He earned his bachelor's degree from Penn State University in 2003 and his master's in journalism from the Medill School of Journalism at Northwestern University in 2008. He also has written for the *Centre Daily Times* (State College, Pennsyvania), *FLYP Media*, the *Washington Post*, *Philadelphia* magazine, *The Guardian* (United Kingdom) and *ESPN the Magazine*. In 2007 Day published his first book, *Along the Tigris: The 101st Airborne Division in Operation Iraqi Freedom*.

Lewis Delavan is a writer for Stephens Media's Arkansas News Bureau in Little Rock. He also has served as an editor for Stephens papers in Hot Springs Village, Arkansas, and Saline County, Arkansas.

Dale Eisman is a veteran reporter and editor based in Washington, D.C., where he was a correspondent for the (Norfolk) *Virginian-Pilot* newspaper from 1994 until 2009. He has covered Virginia state government, state and federal courts, Congress and the Pentagon and traveled with U.S. military personnel on three continents. He is a graduate of Indiana University and a native of Louisville, Kentucky.

Jane Erikson is a former newspaper reporter now working as an independent writer and editor in Tucson. As a reporter, she won numerous state and national awards and honors, mostly for her coverage of health care and social service policy issues. Her honors include the Distinguished Citizen Award from the Arizona Cancer Center.

Ashley Hamershock is a freelance journalist living in Sacramento, California. Previously, she spent several years in Hawaii, freelancing for publications including The Associated Press, *Bloomberg News, Honolulu Magazine, Hawaii Business Magazine* and others. Before that, she spent a decade at The Associated Press in Indianapolis, Minneapolis and St. Paul, most recently as the supervisory correspondent at the Minnesota Capitol.

Tim Holbert is Program Director of the American Veterans Center in Arlington, Virginia. In this capacity, he oversees the Center's documentary and speaker programs, serves as editor of its magazine, *American Valor Quarterly*, and is director of the National Memorial Day Parade. He is host of *Profiles in Valor* on the Radio America network and is writing a book on heroes from Iraq and Afghanistan. He holds B.A. and B.S. degrees from Miami University and a master's degree in economics from George Mason University.

★★★
217
★★★

Tom Lindley is an award-winning writer with an extensive background in newspapers. Lindley has worked for the *New Orleans Times-Picayune, Dallas Times Herald, Wilmington* (Del.) *News Journal* and *The Oklahoman.* He also was the editor of *The Flint* (Michigan) *Journal* for eleven years. Lindley, who is based in Norman, Oklahoma, recently won first-place honors in the Great Plains Journalism Competition for a profile in *Oklahoma Today* magazine.

 Andrew Lubin is an author and independent foreign correspondent who writes on military, economic and geopolitical issues. His work appears regularly in such professional magazines as *Jane's Intelligence Review*, *Leatherneck* and *Proceedings*. He has spent fifteen months embedded with Marine, Army and National Guard troops in Iraq, Afghanistan and Lebanon writing from a "boots on the ground" perspective. His book, *Charlie Battery: A Marine Artillery Battery in Iraq*, won a 2007 Gold Medal from the Military Writers Society of America for best military non-fiction. His Web site is www.andrewlubin.com.

 John Lyon is a reporter covering politics and state government for Stephens Media's Arkansas News Bureau in Little Rock. He has been a reporter for the *Times Record* in Fort Smith, Arkansas, and the *Elk City Daily News* in Elk City, Oklahoma. In his seventeen years as a journalist he has won awards for investigative reporting, reporting on education, feature writing, theater reviews and photography.

 Kevin Maurer has been embedded with the U.S. Special Forces and 82nd Airborne Division in Afghanistan and Iraq more than twelve times in the last six years. Most recently he spent several weeks with a Special Forces team living in a village in central Afghanistan. Maurer's first book about a battle in southern Afghanistan is scheduled to be published next year by Bantam Books. Maurer is a graduate of Old Dominion University in Norfolk, Va. He lives in North Carolina.

 Wesley Millett is a Massachusetts-based freelance writer, historian and author of the acclaimed nonfiction book, *The Rebel and the Rose*, which details the flight of the Confederate government at the end of the Civil War. Millett has written and edited manuals, policy papers and other documentation as a contractor for the U.S. Army and Air Force. He also participates in the annual G.I. Film Festival through promotional activities and interactions with soldiers whose films are being spotlighted during the six-day event.

 Brian Mockenhaupt, a fellow at the Alicia Patterson Foundation, served two tours in Iraq as an infantryman with the 10th Mountain Division. Before joining the Army he worked as a reporter at *The Providence* (Rhode Island) *Journal* and *The* (Phnom Penh) *Cambodia Daily*. Since leaving the Army in 2005, he has written for *Esquire*, *The Atlantic*, *Outside*, *New York Times Magazine* and *Reader's Digest*.